THE GROWING SEASON

the growing season

The Sights and Sounds of Middle Life

MARTHA WHITMORE HICKMAN

Originally published under the title
Love Speaks Its Voice.

THE UPPER ROOM

Nashville, Tennessee

THE GROWING SEASON

Originally published by Word, Inc., under the title
Love Speaks Its Voice

Copyright © 1976 assigned to Martha Whitmore Hickman

Epilogue copyright © 1980 by Martha Whitmore Hickman

First Upper Room printing: September, 1980(5)

Cover transparency by John Netherton

Library of Congress Catalog Card Number: 80-68983

ISBN: 0-8358-0411-9

To the members of my family—
Hoyt, Peter, John, Stephen, and Mary—
in loving acknowledgment of our
common and separate journeys

Contents

An Introduction
I Had Not Planned to Write

Someone has suggested that in every life there is a watershed experience—an event by which time in that life is forever marked, as having taken place before, or after, that significant event. For me—though it is perhaps too soon to tell—that event took place on the midsummer afternoon when my daughter fell from a horse, and died. She would have been seventeen in another two weeks. She was our only daughter and youngest child in a family in which she had been preceded by three sons.

With that event it has seemed to me that the coloration of my life has become radically different—as one would expect, always, when tragedy comes—but almost as though the sky were brown, and the earth blue, or as though the alphabet of our daily life were wrought from different symbols. I have lived through other tragedies, though none so life-violating as this. But with this event it is as though a slash mark was cut through time, my time, and the two worlds, while they have the same cast of characters—even to her, for she is, in a way, still here— and the same locales and, to some extent, the same anxieties and joys—are also different worlds, as if a wall were built across the tunnel of life at that instant. The wall is transparent, but it is sealed to the edges and in the middle of it is her death —as flowers are fixed in a circle of resin. To look back to the events before that death one must look through that resin film; to move in the present at all is to move in the rays projecting from that event.

A week before my daughter's death I had signed a contract to do a book—this book—about some of the events and meanings of middle life. Then she died, and the whole meaning of my life was changed, is changed, is for awhile, thrown into question. How can I write the book for which I had such plans and hopes when the whole sense of my life is violated and I scarcely know who I am anymore, let alone have any confidence to share with others?

9

Slowly, painfully—for I know I must get on with my work—I try to ponder what to do with this event of the death of my daughter. And some voice within me says, bumbling and hesitant, for it knows how fragile my equilibrium is right now—Write it in. Include it. This is the sort of thing that may happen to people in middle life, isn't it?

To people, yes, but not to me, is what I have protested over and over, these past weeks.

That's what they all think, the voice responds.

Yes, I know.

Write it in. Include it. (As though, if I am to do the book at all, I could do anything else.) Be careful, though. You don't want it to be only about her. There are other things you had planned to deal with . . .

I know. I will need to be careful. There are people who can help me, including her. And I can help myself. It will be for me, partly, a way out of despair. It will also be an accounting, a telling about, of how in this wilderness and desolation, bit by haltingly almost incoherent bit, love speaks its voice, life is affirmable even in this so-great loss. The words of a folk-hymn come to mind: "Did you have a new song when you come out the wilderness, come out the wilderness, come out the wilderness?" It *is* a wilderness, and if there is to be a song at all, it has to be a new song, for none of the old songs will do anymore. Will there be a new song, for me?

So, after many weeks of wondering, I get out a piece of blank paper and I roll it into my typewriter—it has been a long time silent. I pause. The moment is heavy with its own freight, of sorrow and threshold and hope. On a strange impulse—it is not my custom, though I read about it once in the work of a writer I admire—I trace the sign of the cross upon my forehead, my chest, my shoulders. I place the palms of my hands together and incline my head slightly toward the rough white walls of the room where I write. It is mime. It is incantation. It is prayer. Let me do it. Help me do it. Let me live.

As a gift I long for but did not expect, I feel a slight lifting of the heaviness, almost an inhalation of the spirit. Am I beginning to trust in a song again?

And I begin.

1

Vocational Shifts,

Role Changes, and

All That

You realize you're in mid-life when:

• You attend three meetings in a row and you suddenly notice how young most of the other people are. . . .

• At these same three meetings you find yourself checking how many people might be older than you. . . .

• You develop a sudden taste for bright, dramatic clothing or a fondness for dim lighting. . . .

• You have to stand on a stool and put the telephone book on the floor in order to read the numbers. . . .

• You tell your eighteen-year-old son that Haile Selassie was Emperor of Ethiopia when you were in fifth grade and he looks incredulous and says, "When *you* were in fifth grade?"

• You read in the paper that in another ten years you'll be eligible for reduced tuition rates at colleges having programs for "older students". . . .

• You begin reading results of national surveys on the frequency of love-making among married couples and are relieved to find you are still above average. . . .

- You realize you get tired more easily than you used to, or your heart pounds if you drink too much coffee.

And the uses of time are so different from what they were—back there—in that other lifetime when the children were small.

It was all so easy back then: get up when the baby cried, feed the family, do the wash, go to the grocery store, keep in touch with your husband, try to leave enough emotional space free so you can be a friend, lover, and consultant for him. Then, there was the share of community things: politics, the church, PTA. After all, everyone was busy and you were competent and had obvious investments in maintaining a decent social order. See, there they are, four of them, running around, eating cookies, scattering parts of puzzles and building sets and doll dishes, falling down and needing comfort, fighting and needing restraint, loving and needing affirmation. Then, if there was a tiny wedge of time left you'd indulge yourself in a painting class or a book group. It was exhausting but bone-satisfying, and if you somehow felt impoverished in the developments of your own gifts you were usually too tired to notice. The choices were simple—do the most demanding thing, then the next most demanding, and so on, until hours and energy gave out.

But time and events do ring their changes and, against all expectations except that of reason, we find that our lives are different. The change does not come overnight, though it has precipitous milestones: the start of the last child to school; the need to set curfew hours and to realize that now you do not need to know where they are all of the time; the acquisitions of drivers' licenses; the departure of the first child for college; and then, the departure of the last.

So the time we have dreaded, and sometimes even, in the early years, longed for, comes. And it is a frontier. Its importance can hardly be exaggerated. We have thought of frontiers in other terms—the physical and geographical events of birth, marriage, a new job, and death. But you can stay at home, in the place where you have lived for twenty years, and still be at a frontier. This may, in fact, be more difficult to deal with because so much seems as it was—the house is the same, the mate is (often) the same, your interests are what they were, the furniture is the same, though less of it is occupied now.

Yes, it is a frontier and it so often comes as a surprise. Why? Who could not see it coming? Can a surprise take five or ten years to happen? We *have* seen it coming. We have read articles about it and thought, yes, I'll be there, too, in a little while. And then suddenly there we are. Looking in the mirror one day we realize that now it is we who are the subject of the articles and are the intended registrants in the continuing education courses. We are those about whom the sociologists talk.

Some aspects of role anxiety at mid-life are common to both men and women. We realize that major changes in vocation— if they are to be made at all—had better be made soon, especially if we have people depending upon us for financial support. My husband and I talked awhile ago with a friend who, approaching forty, has devoted himself to the vocation of art photography. For years now, with the help of his wife whose job has provided them with steady and modest income, he has gotten along. He has had (it seems to us on the outside) a lot of affirmation of his vocation—selling a few prints to a prestigious museum, being given grants and subsidies, publishing one book, then a second and a third, having occasional shows in important galleries. It has been work he could be proud of, could feel to be a genuine fulfillment of his vocation. He has stayed away from commercial photography, which might have helped ease the financial pain, because to do that would, he feared, dull his eye and hand until he would lose his private vision. But now he wonders, should he give it up, be more practical, go into something where he could have a reliable steady income? He is going to be forty and the strain of financial insecurity is becoming harder to bear. He does not say so, but I wonder whether the psychic costs of a free-lance artist do not also seem heavier as the years advance.

Our family goes to visit other friends. The man in the family —he is a math professor in a graduate school—says that he has become interested in autistic children, in meeting the needs of the young. "One has to have a place to do it," he says, some regret in his voice. His oldest son is going through a difficult time. Does this father see his children disappearing from him and, feeling a distance lengthening, long for them again, and another chance? "When I have my second batch of children . . . " my mother-in-law used to say. Do we all wonder whether we could do it better, a second time around? Is there something we could do now, to recoup it all? This is a common speculation of middle life.

My husband and I are sitting with another couple, dear friends, who have come to hike with us on one of the trails in the Colorado mountains. The rain is pouring down and we have taken shelter under an overhanging rock and we get to talking about our goals in life. Jim is a doctor. He has taught in a university medical school and maintained a clinic practice on the side. He is interested in political issues, in getting better health care for the poor, and, yes, he likes the sometime scrappy atmosphere of political life; he is thinking of running for office. Bev, his wife, is a sculptor. Their children are growing up and she has more and more time that she can devote to her art. She has had one show and is going to have another soon. Hoyt, my husband, has recently changed from being a pastor of a local church to working in a denominational headquarters. I am getting more into writing, though I have wondered about other things, too—teaching, social work. All of us are excited about having these options in our lives, though they do not solve all our life anxieties. "Do you think," Bev asks me, "that the switch from motherhood is like retirement?" "No," I reply, "I do not really think so—it is, for one thing, twenty years earlier, but I'm sure they do have some things in common."

Hoyt talks about his mid-career shift. All his vocational life he has had a special interest in worship, in the uses and meanings of ritual. He has been on national commissions on worship, and has written on the subject. A couple of years ago a job became available. "I'm lucky," he says, "that I can do what I want to do." And we know it is true. For many people daily work is an endurance contest—get through the day so you can get out and, for a few hours before you fall asleep from exhaustion or boredom, do something you want to do. The four of us sitting here—we have high expectations. We know we are fortunate.

But it's not all easy, for men or for women, to face these transitions in role and vocation. Often the whole family is affected. What would it be like to have a husband and father in politics? Our family has made a major move from one part of the country to another. The shift from mothering is difficult, too. Our friends are younger than we, their children are still at home. Our three boys have already left home for college. The vocational crisis is upon us in earnest. "I've been feeling very edgy about the whole thing," I say, and am startled to feel tears spring to my eyes. I didn't know I had that much anxiety about it.

What is involved in the vocational crisis of middle life? It is partly a matter of moderating our goals to conform with what is likely to happen. Here may be, at least in terms of past expectations, one important difference between the mid-life strains of men and of women. For women who have been conditioned to think of themselves as prospective, and then actual, wives and mothers, any achievement beyond that is an "extra" —a kind of luxury—though here, as in other situations, our luxuries soon take on the insistence of needs. When I first began to write I thought the sale of one or two articles would satisfy me. Now I want to write books. Men by the same conditioning have traditionally always been more ambitious, more competitive for the choice vocational spots. (If a woman's goal is to be a very successful mother of her own children, she certainly has difficulties but she has no competitors.) But there can be only one president of the company, head of the law firm, foremost expert on Sino-Japanese relations, or bishop of Transylvania. For men at mid-life and, possibly, increasingly so for career-oriented women, too, it may be a modification of goals that is called for, a contentment with relatively modest career achievements.

Women whose vocation has been the raising of children are faced at mid-life with drastic personal change as those children leave home. Recent years have also brought us new messages, both welcome and frightening. Move out, the messages say. Start over. Develop yourself. You can do anything. You aren't satisfied to stay at home and vegetate, you know you aren't! Well, no, of course we don't want to stay home and vegetate, at least not most of the time. I am reminded of a friend who, after a day filled with her job, political involvement, and seeing to the needs of her children said, in an only half-jesting tone, "I want to go home, sit on the sofa, watch television, and waste my life!" But often we don't know what to do, either, as time and events bring the necessity for change. We have, except in those earliest years when time to ourselves seemed the farthest and therefore a very dear possibility, perhaps anticipated the deprivations of our changed status more than its advantages. To have the family at home was what we were used to—it was that that took so much of our day's quota of energy and delight; the freedom we knew would accompany their going was all strange, unfamiliar, and therefore, in some ways frightening. How we would miss them! And in a way it wasn't fair that, having seen them through chicken pox, braces, adolescent acne, and the emotional strains of growing up, we should have them suddenly cut out and leave home for good.

There may have been an element of fear of ourselves, too, in our dread of their leaving. For so many years so much of our life-energy has gone to them and, yes, we have known the dangers of finding our identity in those roles of being wife and mother and have tried to keep an eye on that, but there they were, and there we were, and it was very satisfying to feel so needed, to take joy in being their mother and being proud of them. Now, when they are about to go, what is left of me? Am I interesting, resourceful, worthwhile, good company for myself? Will the ghosts of old fears come back to plague me now that I have so much more emotional time and space available for occupancy? Will my life anxiety, my "world pain"—those voices of disquietude that plague me from time to time—become louder and more demanding? Who shall I be? Will I know myself at all? Will I like myself, or not? What shall I do with my time? The day holds many hours, what shall I do with the time?

Edwin Land, the developer of the Polaroid Land Camera, in an address before the Cosmos Club in Washington, D.C., describes the human person as needing to move back and forth between two states of being—one where the person exists as part of a group, as a social person and, the other, a state of being that is essentially solitary, needing to do its own work—an integration inward that is quite free of social pulls upon it. He suggests that unless we can make these migrations back and forth, and keep our lives in good balance, we shall not be whole.

As I have thought about this in regard to the vocation of motherhood, it occurs to me that for many women there is a period of *years* when only the social being can operate—what mother of small children can on any regular basis pull herself away from her family to do her sustained privately integrating work? So maybe we lose the skill for those inward migrations, and when at last we do have time, our muscles for solitude are stiff and we turn to the easier thing, which is to replace the flurry of childcare with other flurries of social groups, of giving ourselves to others—the old, the sick, the young, the troubled. These are splendid good works but they need to be balanced with times of dropping a plumb line down and finding out what, in our solitude, our *ownness*, we are like. It may be frightening, after years of being poured out for other persons, to stop long enough to look at what it is we are now pouring out; but if we do not, we may face a kind of continual abdication of our own presence, a running away from ourselves which takes the risk of aloneness away but may take much of the savoring of life away, too.

So, who shall I be? What shall I do with the hours when the balance shifts and the few volunteer activities and hobbies are no longer what I do with "the rest of the time," and I must somehow reshape the vocational agenda of my life?

Often we enter much more fully into a "flounder stage," where we cast about for new vocations and new identity. We may try out some rather frantic "busy work": compulsive housekeeping, elaborate cooking, sewing on a wardrobe which comes to far exceed our needs, afternoons of bridge and shopping. We may start going to more of the civic, religious, and cultural meetings most communities offer in abundance. We may even become involved in the supercharged mindlessness of daytime television. Some of these activities are fine. But we need to be careful, to know what we are doing.

We may in our journey through the "flounder stage," try some volunteer work in a more ambitious way: helping at a Headstart center, visiting prisoners in jail, helping transport senior citizens back and forth to the doctor. Often we will try several of these before we find the combination of skill, time, and involvement that seems right for us. I had been a free-lance writer for a number of years and yet, with my children gone, found the need for some regular meaningful exchange with people apart from my family and friends. I tried several things—considered belonging to a speakers' bureau on issues of discrimination and inclusion. But that took mostly evenings, time when I could be with my husband. I began on a training program for volunteers to go to public school with a presentation for children aimed at enlarging their empathies for outsiders and appreciating the variety of the human family. After two sessions I wrote the director to say I was dropping out—a lot of preparation time would be necessary, schedules would be variable, and it didn't seem right for me. Then I tried an afternoon a week at a crisis call center—an emergency telephone service where people in need could call and talk with a sympathetic and trustworthy person who would also know the resources of the community. Sometimes the talking was all the callers needed. Sometimes they needed referral to an agency that could help with food, housing, counselling. I went at twelve, and I left at three, and the work did not follow me home. I felt needed, successful in my efforts and warmed by the human interchange.

I feel the need to sound a word of warning, though, about volunteer work as a long-term solution to the problem of role change in mid-life. We have learned much from the women's movement about the hazards of volunteerism. Much of it we have known in our bones for a long time, which is why it makes such sense to us now. Our society, with notable exceptions, gives us the message—if it is worthwhile, it is worth paying for. A woman who is already feeling insecure—a bit superfluous because she is not needed at home any more—often does not get a whole lot of affirmation of herself at a time when she needs it most, particularly if she sees that other people do many of the things she is doing, but they are getting paid for it. Therefore, her reading of the message will say she must not be worth as much as they are. It is one of society's dilemmas that, on the one hand, there are things that desperately need doing that there is no money to pay for and that have their value enhanced because someone is doing them out of concern rather than because he or she is paid to do them, and, on the other hand, the need of women—who have traditionally been the largest pool of volunteers—to feel they are worthwhile in the terms in which society operates. There are certainly women who are mature and whole enough to be volunteers in spite of all this but, as with any other instance of living in counterthrust to society's messages, we had better know what we are doing.

In this "flounder stage" we have, particularly in recent years, had many who are ready to help us. In the city where I live I have received, within a span of several days, brochures for two symposia on women's role in society—one, run by the local university on "Choice and Change for Women," the other, on "Women in a New Community," offered by the center for continuing education of a small college. In the morning paper I read an announcement that the Woman's Civic Forum is sponsoring a talk on "Women in Search of Self" and a recent Sunday newspaper supplement ran a long article on an upcoming series of talks by community leaders to help women find their places as volunteer workers in community agencies. Another article describes a conference on the more specialized problems of women whose children have grown, and alludes to the loneliness and depression that often go with "life-style changes when the children from whom, the woman drew her identity depart and she has nothing to replace them." The list goes on, until you wonder what women talked about before the women's movement helped us to bring so much of this into focus. You wonder whether it will be easier for our daughters to get these things sorted out than it sometimes seems to be for us.

The university in our city has recently established a career counseling office for women in middle life. I wonder—maybe that would help me sort out some of my own vocational questions. I make an appointment and go and talk with the director.

We talk about the options for women and then about the options for me. There are ways in which I know writing to be my vocation, but it is often lonely, and right now I am not sure. Maybe a part-time job? We talk about education, job experience, possible job opportunities. She lends me booklets on teaching, on social work and counseling—obvious channels for women who have been "helping persons" for so long. She gives me a booklet containing self-evaluation tests.

I go home, take the tests, and try to evaluate them. I talk too much to my husband and daughter about what-am-I-going-to-do-now and they listen and are sympathetic and they know, as I do, that it is *I* who must decide.

Every morning, along with my coffee and the last segment of the morning news, I read the want-ads in the paper: Employment: management-professional; skilled and semi-skilled; general help wanted. I hope I find something interesting. I hope I don't.

The weeks go by. In the mornings I write. I am working on an article and I have in mind revising the long manuscript I finished last spring. I see friends. I keep reading the employment ads in the paper and I call about an occasional job that looks interesting. I continue to wonder about the uncertainty and loneliness of writing and whether the satisfactions are worth the cost.

Months pass, events come and go and one day I realize that for me, the "flounder stage" is over. I have an afternoon job now, not through answering want-ads, but through a friend who knew of the job and thought I might be interested. I enjoy the work—a kind of research and telephone consultation work that is very demanding when I am there but asks nothing from me after I leave. I like the people I work with. My job provides some structure and balance to my life at a time when I need these badly. Most important, my writing is going well and I have enough confidence to continue.

So, for awhile the choice of "what now?" is made. My life has sorted itself out, has "settled." But no, wait, it did not "sort itself out." *I* sorted it out, with the help and support of my husband, children, friends, community agencies, and some good luck. That is something, too, that women must come to terms with—that we and not our husbands or society or our children must take responsibility for what we do with our lives. We may not be able to have our first choices, but we should at least realize it is we who must take charge of whatever revelations come, whatever resolutions to the floundering occur.

This taking charge, this evaluating and studying and deciding, demands a lot of us and it may not come easily after so many years of taking our cues from others. The journey from being a mother whose children have all left home and who feels somewhat lost, unneeded, at loose ends, to being someone who feels secure in new vocations, new interests, and who feels the excitement and growth in all that—is not easy, and who of us knows whether she has made the right turns in the road.

But maybe we do know. Thoreau puts it: "If the day and the night are such that you greet them with joy, and life emits a fragrance like flowers and sweet-scented herbs, is more elastic, more starry, more immortal—that is your success." A friend of mine has said, in talking about vocation, "I think you know when you're in the will of God." And another, "Your body will tell you when you're not doing the right thing." Our bodies give us many messages to indicate we are somehow at variance with ourselves and things are not dovetailing right—sleeplessness, digestive upsets, functional high blood pressure, a tendency of overeating. Our bodies will help us, too, through a sense of poise and well-being, to know what our vocation *is*.

It may seem one-sided, egocentric, in view of "the needs of the world," to put so much reliance on our own emotional barometers. Should we not use more rational considerations? We do need to use our reasoning power, of course, in evaluating skills, markets, and resources. We need to be aware of the lure of the familiar because it is familiar and of the new because it is new, and to weigh those things as best we can. But when we have done that, and are faced with deciding among the several things we could probably do, what is there but our own sense of being at home with ourselves to tell us which is right?

A friend with whom I was talking about this told me how her academic career was at a crisis point. She had taught in a university the prescribed number of years and now she was up for tenure. "If I don't get it," she said, "I have thought to myself, What shall I do? Do something other than teach? And then I realized, that's what I am, a teacher." She looked at me —I had been telling her of my own uncertainties—that the needs of my life had changed and maybe I should look for something completely different. "The same is true about you," she said. "You are a writer."

For my friend, as for me, it is this feeling of being at home with one's self that validates our vocation. It cannot be overstressed. It is more important than new batches of excitement, or someone else's evaluation of social value, or more important than the need to develop extra skills. This sense of being at home with one's self may not be available to us when we are young, but by the time we have reached middle age it is the last arbiter of vocational choice. It is not, surely, the only arbiter, but when all the other weights are on the scale, it is that sense of being at home with the self that really counts.

Having said all this, we must recognize that among the world's people, we who are free to decide among opportunities for work, are among the privileged few. For many people the subtleties of vocational choice are lost beyond a barrier of what-shall-I-do-to-survive. That knowledge, too, is part of our stewardship of choice—if we are privileged to have the power to choose our work, let us do it well, with care, with abandon, with love.

After we have gone through our dreads, our anticipations and worries, our floundering and our (relative) settling, what do we find? We probably discover, if we have proceeded well, that the advantages of "the empty nest" stage are real—there is more to be said for it than our old suspicion that it was a cheer-up-and-make-the-best-of-it means of dealing with a difficult situation. We do have time. Our energy lights on different things and finds them good. We can go away for the weekend without worrying about the children back home. Two can eat out or go to the movies much more cheaply than six. And to be alone with one's husband again and free from preoccupation with the children can be the occasion for new experiences in shared interests, in intimacy, in mutual growth. One also has time at last to meet a friend for lunch, to read, to go for a swim, to sit in the sunshine and feel how good it is on the back of the neck, to act on impulse and go to an intriguing meeting just to see what it's like.

There is also a strange kind of freedom which life hands us at this stage in our development. It is the sense of being, in a way, expendable, and therefore, perhaps, more at ease with the fragility of life. When our children are young and so obviously dependent upon us for emotional and physical well-being, the responsibility for all that may make us fearful. What if something happened to me? Of course if something happened to me now—if I died—the people who love me would mourn for me, and of course had I died when the children were small someone could have done for them, been for them, some of the things I did and was; but they are more independent now, they are safely launched, and while I certainly do not court death I am relieved to know these children are grown and ably responsible to handle their own lives. I have other work to do, other persons who depend on me, but it is not the same, and the freedom inherent in that situation helps me to relax into my life and to enjoy the quality of the relationships I now have. The weight of the world was never on my shoulders, but sometimes it felt as though it were. It doesn't feel that way, any more.

I must also mention two other aspects of role and vocation and then I am done. "If I am not the mother of these children, who am I?" Ah, but I am. They are grown, they do not need me as they did. But until I die and even should they precede me in death, I am their mother. Nothing that was, is lost. It is with me in fact, in memory, in the history in which my life is wrought. I am different things to them now than I was fifteen years ago. I am still their mother, by biology and our common past, and that is inviolate. So often we forget that. Let us remember. Whatever was, is ours still. It is fused to us, it is an irremovable treasure.

The other thing has to do with the nature of vocation as Being rather than as Doing, and it, too, is a constant with us all our lives. Let us nurture our being now, for the nowness of it, and also in the hope that we are preparing for our quieter years, so that when we are old, it will not depart from us.

2

Our Place and Where We Feel at Home

"Life is an affair of people not of places," Wallace Stevens wrote. "But for me, life is an affair of places and that is the trouble." This is a favorite quotation of mine, though perhaps it overstates the case. And yet we, sometime heirs of an impossible dualism between physical and spiritual, often try to tell ourselves that the places where we are, the houses we live in, the streets we live along, and the colors and shapes with which we surround ourselves somehow should not matter so much. They matter.

All we have to do to know how much they matter is to move —even to contemplate moving. At the mere suggestion that we might be moving, the internal sorting begins—What shall I take with me? What can I leave behind that I would be happy to do without? What feature of this house—a fireplace, an attic, a corner window—must I have in another house? What is of secondary importance? Where will the pictures go? Will the blue of the new sofa fit with the colors of a new house? Will my rosebushes transplant? What shall I do about the old bed in the attic?

The Growing Season

To be sure, not everyone moves, and perhaps among the infinite ways of categorizing the inhabitants of the world, one of the more credible ways would be to divide us all into those who move and those who don't. I have a friend who is now retiring and is still living in the house in which he was born. My own history of staying was not that long, but my conditioning was of one who did. I lived in one house all my remembered childhood and my mother lives there now.

We who are stayers share a common mystique about our long-rootedness. I think of a cousin, a man many years my senior. We were engaged in conversation, trying politely to deal with our vast differences in political points of view. The tension in that conversation suddenly dissipated when we started to talk about *place*. He looked around the yard of his home, at the gardens down the hill where he had planted his vegetables, at the gentle slope of the land, and I could see him caress it with his eyes. "I know every blade of grass on this place," he said. "If you haven't lived in one place for a long time you just can't understand what that means." "I know," I said. "I understand."

The artist Andrew Wyeth says in defense of his habit of going to only two places—to Maine in the summer and back to Pennsylvania in the winter—"The familiar frees me." I understand that, too, and having moved several times in the early years of our marriage, I know the difference between moving and staying. I know that when you move it takes a long time before you are freed from the bondage of newness and the need to put so much energy into all the accommodations to newness and can get on with perceiving sunshine and love and trees for sunshine and love and trees.

Most of us by middle life have done some of both—some moving, some staying. Often in mid-life we move again, as the company moves us to our peak achievement niche, or as our vocational interests take a last important major shift.

To move in middle life presents again the occasion for examining what our place means to us, and what we need and do not need at this time in our lives. Our family, after my husband's years in graduate school, early pastorates, and then after a stay in one house for eight years made a major move, from Pennsylvania to Tennessee. All the anxieties and challenges of a move at that time of life showered down upon us. How would it be for our children? (Hardly children any more). Two of our boys were out of high school—one half way through college and one about to begin. Would they have any sense of "home" about a place they returned to only for vacations? Would they feel any ties to the new community, so far in miles, climate, and culture from anything they had known? Would they want to go there, except for perhaps dutiful visits to see their parents? What about the two children who would be in high school in the new city? Would they make the adjustments all right? Our third son would be a senior, a notoriously poor time to move. And our daughter, who had a spiritual affinity between herself and certain places of the state in which she was born—how would it be for her, to pick up and leave it all, the places, her girlfriends, the boy friend with whom she spent time almost daily? Would she—beautiful, blossoming, with a gift for friendship but with her share of adolescent insecurities, too—would she be lonely and unhappy? And my husband and I. . . . We were delighted at this new turn in life, but how would it be for us? My vocational tools are easy to move, but the rest of it, the friends and associations—how would that be?

The choice of a house! Am I alone, or does every woman in the world find that at a time of moving the choice of a house is a concern that for awhile seems to take up almost all the emotional landscape? We put impossible demands on a house and the choice of it, until we realize that perhaps we are *not* sealing our eternal destiny by the choice of the dwelling we and our family will inhabit.

But for awhile it seems that way—at least for me. Perhaps it was because this was our first experience in choosing our own house. We had lived in parsonages before. So now, with our family nearly grown, we came to this occasion of choosing a home. What about the space we would need—a house big enough for everyone to come home to, and yet not so large that when, in a few years, there would be only two of us living here all the time, we would feel we were rattling around in an empty shell? Could we accept, in our choice of a house, the realities of the changes in our lives? A woman I talked with about her own choice of a house now that two of her three children were grown, told me how she wanted a house big enough for them all to come home to, and "to come home to comfortably." I sympathized with that, but I wondered whether it was not also an attempt to deny that her children were, in fact, growing up and leaving home.

Not only the needs for space change, but time and energy may seem more precious. One of the houses we considered buying was an older home with rambling hallways and larger rooms than the house we finally chose. It was a lovely house, but it needed a lot of work—a new furnace, kitchen and laundry renovations, a central air conditioning system. Completed, it would have cost no more than the house we did choose. Ten years ago, the project might have been fun, but now it would have taken so much time and energy to do all the investigating, make all the decisions, and live through the renovation upsets. We felt we were too old, that time and energy were too precious to consign all of that to getting our nest right for us. I thought of that choice again a few days ago when I was in a fabric store and overheard parts of a conversation between the sales clerk and a young woman of about thirty. She and her husband—she explained it all at length—were planning some kind of extensive wall decoration. They needed some long poles, and some decorative ends for the poles, and some supports for them, and some material to make sheer curtains and some more material to make valances and draperies. I was tired just thinking about it, and I realized that she stood at a different point in life than I. Fifteen years ago I could have been very excited at such an undertaking, making all those careful calculations and doing all the planning and sewing and hanging. But now I see that I do not have endless time and energy at this stage in my life. I need to put mine to other tasks.

What *do* we need, now or at any time, from the places where we live? Part of what we are looking for—and it is important to realize this when no house seems quite adequate, quite right —is something that never did exist as timber and brick and glass, and is therefore not to be found at all, not now. I refer to that larger-than-life security we felt or, in retrospect, believe that we felt, in those hallowed rooms and hallways and closets and back porches where we spent our childhood years. How snug they were—that space behind the couch where as small children playing "house" we staked out our territory, or the front hall closet which, with the coats pushed back and the light turned on and with a few papers, crayons, doll dishes, and items of cast-off finery became a place of infinite coziness. Conversely, how big it all was—the house we remember—how splendid, a castle almost! (Have you gone and looked at it lately? Do you dare?) It was not until a couple of years ago when we moved to Tennessee and I was at last able to transfer some of the roots of "home" from Massachusetts to our new home, that it even occurred to me to try to look at my parents' house as though I were a stranger to it. It was still a lovely house—the blue and white pattern of the wallpaper in the living room, the oriental rugs on the floor, the bookcases filled with unfathomed mysteries loved and unread, the family pictures, the light streaming in through the windows onto the chair by the cherry table—they were all there, reflections of my parents' tastes and of all our lives. But somehow the room was not as large as I had thought. Why, my tall sons and daughter, stretched out along the floor, took up most of the available floor space between chairs and sofa, between the fireplace and the table where, of a late Sunday afternoon, I would raise the dropped leaf, pull up a chair and, in the light of the lamp with the mosaic parchment shade, do my homework.

What I wanted in my own house was a room as big, as filled with light and magic, as my oversized memory of my parents' living room, and at the same time as snug and cozy as that hall closet, or the house I made for myself from a blanket draped over a cardtable. Such a mix never existed, and the security or imagined security of childhood, or the perspective that turns modest living rooms into palace ballrooms, are not to be found in adult habitation. But we look for them, want them for our children who must, after all, make their own palaces.

What do we need from a house—knowing that the places where we live not only express us but continue to shape our lives? I have read that men see their houses as territories, women, as extensions of their bodies. I wonder whether that is so and how it relates to the cultural messages we receive about ourselves. What do we need? My husband, having lived in a handsome house with large grand rooms, wants a house that is "cozy." I want to be sure the rooms are spacious enough. The boys, offered the choice of piling all three of them into one room—which was their arrangement in the house we lived in before—or dividing up and one of them taking the fourth bedroom, opt to stay together, though that choice might be different were two of them not going to be away at college most of the time. Mary, rejoicing in the large corner window of her room, chooses orange for her decor, surrounds herself with plants, and wants her bed put so that when she wakes up she can see the trees outside her window. My husband and I, sharing so much of our lives with each other, are delighted that, again, we shall each have a closet of our own.

In the room where I write are rough white walls, grooved with vertical boards, and a window wall facing out onto the patio and the trees I have come to love. I have set my desk so the window wall is behind me—I cannot afford to be distracted. But the light streams in through it, and I can rotate my swivel chair to look out and see the life that teems out there and feel my kinship with grass and trees, with birds and squirrels.

On one of the white grooved walls of the room I have hung many pictures of our children—baby pictures, high school pictures, casual shots showing them with backpacks and cameras, doing the things that they love to do. I want them in the room with me, but not within my normal viewing range as I sit at my desk. In this place, at this stage in my life, I need to be about other things than the contemplation of my children.

I do have three things hanging near my desk, where my glance falls upon them often. One is a card on which a poem by Bernard Gunther is superimposed on a gray and white painting by Corita Kent. The card was sent to us by some friends after the death of our daughter, and it is about being able to love yourself, to let go of the past, to live in the present moment. It is a message I need at any time, but coming as it did it was a particular gift and I like to have it where I can see it often. The other card taped on the wall was sent to me many months ago. It tells me that, because of my inclusion in one of the less prestigious reference books of noteworthy women, I have been selected for inclusion in a "Library of Human Resources." I am charmed at the notion. For $15 I can have a beautiful parchment certificate proclaiming myself as a Human Resource. I certainly do not want the certificate. But I am often uneasy about myself and knowing full well that my inclusion as a Human Resource is more of an effort to make money from my potential vanity than it is a designation of merit—still, I hang up my card with a mixture of bemusement and pride. It is nice to be considered a Human Resource (especially in capital letters).

The third item on the wall is an envelope, which I have framed, sent to us by one of our sons at college. He tells us that he did the beautifully elaborate calligraphy on the envelope as a way of putting off writing the letter. It is a work of art—scrolls, flowers, little faces, and branching leaves surrounding our surname, the number and name of the street where we live, the city, the state and yes, with trailing flourishes, the five digits of our zip code. It hangs there on the wall, a kind of talisman of location. I like to look at it and to think of my son, his head inclined over his desk, his deft hands moving with the intricate tracery of his work.

We make social as well as personal statements about ourselves when we choose the place of our dwelling. My mother, past eighty, shares with me her vulnerability of more than sixty years ago when she tells how her parents, faced with the need to make a sudden move, had thought that maybe they would establish a summer home on an island, but—in a tent. She was away at college, she says, when the decision was made and, being the first of her family to attend college, may have already been struggling with questions of self-image in a community that included the very affluent as well as people of modest means. "When they told me that," she says, her voice reflecting a kind of childlike honesty as well as some chagrin that she must have put pressure on her already beleaguered parents, "I was quite disappointed." She paused for a minute, and I could feel the ambivalence she must have felt way back then, not wanting to conceive of herself as a young woman who lived in a tent, even if only for a summer, and yet feeling ashamed that what should seem acceptable to her parents, should seem unacceptable to her. She continued, "Then my father built the camp"—a place I remembered with great affection, and so did she—a place with rooms, a kitchen, a porch, established wooden sides, and a roof, like a proper dwelling.

The house we live in rambles off to the side and the back in adventurous form. From the street the house looks rather small. I am torn with feelings about that—yes, I want it to look "as big as it is," though I am chagrined that this is so. On the other hand, in a way I am glad our house looks smaller than it is, self-conscious as I am about relative affluence and buying a house in an almost-suburb. If I wish, occasionally, for a more impressive façade and a living room where sixteen people could sit and not feel crowded, I remember our friends Paul and Selma who have gone to live in a Christian commune. Paul's skills as an architect are directed toward building small private living quarters and then larger common areas, as a way of acting out the community of faith.

Where we live identifies us not only to others, but to ourselves. Visiting in Israel, I see the refugee camps where, for generations now, families have lived as permanent transients —row after row of concrete squares set on barren land, crowded together. I wonder, How do they think of themselves, with this feeling of uprootedness which grandfathers have passed on to children, who have never lived other than here? Do they feel, "This is my home and yet I am not supposed to feel at home here?" My friend from the Ukraine tells us how her parents had to leave their possessions behind and flee. They now live over a shabby church in an industrial town. They are glad to be alive. Her father, proclaiming his faith, has a radiant face; her mother looks drawn and sad. To what use can she put her loss? If I find my security shaken by moving a thousand miles, within my own country, my things in a big van following me here, what must it be like for her?

So, in middle life, I move. My first house. Our first house. The children like it. I am immeasurably grateful. Our furniture is slow in coming but we have two living room chairs and each morning I sit in the almost empty room and, my coffee cup in my hand, look out through the big corner window at the mimosa tree and savor what it is like to feel at home here.

I am eager for my parents, my brother and sisters, to come, to give sanction to our house. There is a blue glass compote rimmed with gold that stands on a bookcase in my parents' house. My father and I have shared a fondness for that high-stemmed bowl. "I like that color blue," he said to me once, years ago. It has been one of our common affinities for a long time. In the guestroom of our house I have put bedspreads with that color blue against a white background, and on the windowsill I put the blue vase of exactly that color which, a few years ago, my daughter, uninformed but knowing, bought for me on one of the many occasions of her generosity.

I wait for my father to come and see them. He and my mother plan to come for the first Thanksgiving in our house and I have thought how I will take him, also a lover of place, to the areas of special presence in my house and stand with him there. But he cannot come. A few days before they are to leave they call me—his health has been frail and he does not feel he can make the trip—maybe later he will feel strong enough. Within a week he is in the hospital and though he lives for six more months he never returns to his strength, and part of my sorrow at the prospect of the loss of my father is the knowl-edge that he will not stand with me by the corner window and watch the cardinals and squirrels that chirp, scamper, and flit in the trees outside; that he will not sleep in the room with the blue and white bedspreads and the vase on the windowsill. I take him pictures of the house but he is scarcely able to enter into that with me, there in the hospital room. His energy goes to his being with me, and to his own house where for almost fifty years he has lived among the spaces, walls, light, and people of his own most cherished world.

My father cannot come, but a year later, my mother comes. My husband's family, my sisters, my friends from Boston, all come to visit. We show them our house expectantly and we hang onto their every word of commendation—of the house's physical qualities yes, but of its spiritual reflections, too—the flow of light, the way rooms open up onto other rooms and wander off where one did not expect them—acting out what we would like to believe about ourselves—that we are people of wide-ranging interests and even a bit of mystery.

We "get used to" our house and yard. We adjust to the blazing heat of summer and are grateful for the air condition-ing. I sit in the backyard in the late evening and, take in the sounds and smells of the southern night—the crickets and cicadas, the lushness of green things growing. In the north we had to keep encouraging things to grow, here the task is to keep them trimmed back or they will take over. To my surprise and delight, I realize that I who have thought myself so rooted in New England that I would always feel a stranger somewhere else, feel at home here. One day, in a sudden burst of affirmation, the vine on the patio wall bursts into bloom and turns out to be—wisteria! My childhood home had a wisteria vine climbing to the sleeping porch—how many summer nights have I gone to sleep in the fragrance and companionship of those flowers? The wisteria vine, blooming here against the white-washed brick, tells me, you were right. This is the right house for you. You are home.

Where shall we go from here? Or shall we stay in this house until we die? We do not need to know, yet the prospect of those decisions come to mind. Our parents are still in the large houses in which they raised their families. I know there are other options. Some dreary, some good. There is a knoll in western Pennsylvania, the second highest point in Allegheny County. It is included in some acreage on which the first Hickmans to come to this country, in 1753, established their farm. The land is still owned by a family descendant. My husband and I have speculated about that. If we had the money, and that land became available, would we like to build a small home there for our retirement? We could build a workroom apiece for us and lots of glass wall for the sweeping view from that hilltop. Or would that be too unprotected a spot for us, when we are old? My family's roots go back for generations into New England. Is there some hallowed spot up there where we might want to live?

A professor friend of my son's tells him how he and his wife and his sisters and their husbands have tentatively planned that when they all retire they will establish a kind of family commune—small homes for each of them, close together, close to a university center, close to medical facilities. They have already found the part of the country where they want to set up their family preserve—in a semi-rural region close to a cluster of colleges in New England. It comforts me to think of such an arrangement, fond as I am of my own siblings and feeling already the foreshadowing chill of the possible loneliness of old age. My son, also fond of his siblings and just out of college and feeling a kind of loneliness, brings me this information as a glad possibility—for himself and for my husband and me. I am grateful.

There is something else about having lived in this succession of homes and that is the realization that for the person who moves and stays and moves and stays and moves again—there is a sense in which, in the midst of all this, *I* am my home. Like a turtle who carries her shell above and beneath her I carry in my body and my consciousness, my home. I am not very brave about this, knowing how I need other people and the places of my security, but I have lived long enough, been through enough, to believe, to hope that I am competent and faithful enough and imbued—by God, by good experiences, and some irrepressible autonomy which is myself—with enough generating power that wherever I find myself I will be able to call out my name, to reestablish my connections, and to be at home. This confidence was not mine when I was younger. I suppose the need for it had not occurred to me, located as I felt to a particular spot and the dislocation from that spot seeming like some unnatural violation. It is not always with me now. But it is a hope I have, helped by knowing that there are ways in which I carry the histories of my places with me—the sunlit room of my childhood, a particular grove of trees with a particular stream afloat with watercress—and also by having, over quite a few years, felt at home in places which had been strange to me—either over a period of months, as I feel at home now in the south, or in a fleeting but nonetheless real way, as because of past associations known and unknown I feel at home immediately.

I think of standing by the Dead Sea and looking over at Mount Nebo and remembering how my father used to read to me, "By Nebo's lonely mountain, On this side Jordan's wave, In a vale in the land of Moab, There lies a lonely grave . . ." and realizing that somehow, in an interior way, I had appropriated that place as my own, so that now, forty years and thousands of miles away, I felt at home.

In a strangely paradoxical way, the ability to feel that wherever I am, I am my home, helps me to believe that the universe

35

is my home—that somehow I who live in this body of muscle and bone and fluid, of will and anxiety and joy, have a kinship with all that is.

This came to me in a special way one day two summers ago when our family was concluding a week of family reunion-vacation in the lake area of northern Wisconsin. The week had been rich with common adventure and association and now the eighteen of us who had been together were going to go off to our four distant homes. I had awakened early and feeling rather vulnerable and lonely, full of "last day" feelings, had got up and gone alone to the end of the dock jutting out from our shore.

Standing on the dock I saw a spider web strung out between the poles of a wire brace holding the dock posts in place. The web was large and the wind was blowing through it, but it did not break, its strength, flexibility, and the openness of the web allowing the wind to pass through it, and I thought how I would like to be as able to receive the wind and as resilient as that web. I got into a rowboat and rowed out past a fisherman who looked at me warily, and went into a nearby cove, where I rested my oars. The water was clear, the grassy weeds a beautiful green. The sounds of morning on the water came to me. Birds and bugs skimmed the water, alone or in consort, chasing one another. A lone bird perched on a blackened branch high above my head. Feeling again that kind of free-floating loneliness, related, I suppose, to the coming breakup of our family reunion, I thought to myself, Will I ever leave this vulnerability behind, so I do not feel stripped to my nerve-endings, exposed to every shift of feeling and sensibility? And something within me said, Is that what you really want? and I said, No. Well, then . . . and that was when it came to me—a revelation of the grass and water as my kin. That I am not "over against" all of it, but I am part of it, organically tied to it, and we, these green things, this morning sun that calls the bugs and birds back into life—we nourish one another. I, them, and they, me. A peace came over me then and some of the anguish went. I felt it leaving, as a vapor moving over the water, and the clouds which were beginning to collect and cover the sun seemed warm and friendly, too.

I sat for a moment, enjoying the sun and the skimming birds

and the clear morning air. I would go back. I turned the boat in my cove, and rowed back to shore. The boat ground up on the beach and I walked back the boat's length and stepped out on the watery sand and secured the ropes to a post. I looked up toward one of our family's cottages high on the hillside and through the window I saw my sister and my mother watching me. They waved, and I waved back and went up to join them.

Months later, after my daughter died and I had been forced to reexamine my whole sense of the love of God and the meaning of my life against pain and anger and a loss from which surcease does not come, I thought of my morning in the cove and wondered, Can I still feel a kinship with the energy and flow of the world? I who have felt a kind of unfathomable life rejection in the death of my daughter?

Not easily, not constantly, not without travail and pain, and the help of friends who can imagine no more than I how it is possible to believe in life when one is so confronted with death but who, in that knowledge, reach out to help me, I am able to say, haltingly and with a residue of anger still in the back of my throat, Yes. Yes, I believe that. Yes. There is something worth trusting, even in all of this. "I do not see," a friend says to me, "how that can come about except by grace." "Nor do I," I say, and for a moment we are silent before this mystery.

Being at home. I have been at home in many places and loved them, and I carry them in my mind, for comfort and delight. I find new homes, and shall, in places I have not yet come upon. Now, in the middle of my life, released into speculations and freedoms both welcome and terrifying, I think about being at home, and what that means to me. H. Richard Niebuhr, in a marvelous passage in *The Responsible Self*, talks about the message of indifference which sometimes seems to be written into the universe but how Christians, struggling with that are able to say at least from time to time and by some miracle of grace set forth by Christ—No, that's not how it is, there's something going on which we trust, something which seems, even in the midst of death and sorrow, to bubble up with grace, with love. It is a different assumption, Niebuhr says, from much that we see around us which holds that life must ultimately be viewed with despair. No, the Christian says, That's not how it is. I cannot prove it to you, I can tell you only that my life has a different infusion, is played against a different background music. We do not live in this assurance always, in any continuous victory over fear. But the hunches continue to come, to break through and spread a kind of grand delight—a great Aha! over our lives—a sense of having come to our place. "We were," Niebuhr says, "blind in our distrust of being, now we begin to see; we were aliens and alienated in a strange, empty world, now we begin sometimes to feel at home."

To feel at home in the universe—it is like going into your house in the darkness and finding that someone you love has already turned on the lights.

3

The Changing

Varieties of

Parenthood

A few years ago our family of six was on a weeklong trip through northern New England. It was a nostalgic "last fling" for us because we all knew in a way it was the end of a world. In a few weeks our oldest son would start to college and that knowledge shadowed and sharpened all the marvelous variables of the week. He did most of the driving. We all enjoyed the rough timber roads of northern Maine—the wild scenery of the woods and then the crags, white spume, and incredible blue sky along the east coast at Bar Harbor where, in the beginnings of cold twilight we swam in the surf until our hands and legs grew numb and we felt we had been in long enough to say we had swum off the coast of Maine.

One of the rich moments of our trip came at the end of a day when, after searching and passing up several motels, we finally found one in this resort country that did not have a No Vacancy sign posted outside. But from this last try my husband returned and said, "They have one room, with two double beds, and they have one cot left that they can put in the room," to which the other members of our family of six said with one voice, "We'll take it."

The Growing Season

We got in the room, and it was as though we had acquired a palace—it was clean, it had airconditioning, a shower, a television set, and only one too few beds. And it was a place of our own. We were secure. We went out to get some food and improvised a sixth sleeping place from some chair cushions laid out on the floor and sat around on the various surfaces for awhile. Then by careful logistics we got everyone into sleeping clothes and there we were—wall-to-wall people, tired, content, jocular—in an intimate-family mood and before we turned off the lights, the television and the chitchat, we listened to the eleven o'clock news and from our various positions of unaccustomed and soon-to-be-asleep closeness, heard with particular delight the familiar words of the announcer, "It's eleven o'clock. Do you know where your teen-aged children are tonight?" Ah yes, we knew, we knew. Could we not reach out and touch them, every one?

It is one of my favorite stories, and I think one of the reasons it appeals to me so much is that it was such a reassuring symbol —everyone together, close, safe, feeling good about one another, at a time of life when the pressure is toward an explosion *out* into the world.

I think of more harried scenes, perhaps more typical of families at this stage, like the several variations on the why-isn't-he-home-yet? theme. I remember a particularly snowy night when John, who had recently learned to drive, and who had gone to a party at the home of a friend, had not arrived home by the legal and family curfew hour of midnight. By 12:10 I was pacing the floor and Hoyt, reading a magazine, was looking at his watch but pretending not to. My exchange with John that afternoon—"When will you be home, dear?"—"Oh, I suppose around midnight." "OK"—had become in fantasy, "I don't want you ever to go away from me and if you do, please, please be home by five of twelve if not two hours sooner." By 12:20 Hoyt and I were into an exchange that ran something like this:

M: How can you sit there and read that magazine when John may be in desperate shape somewhere? I wish you would call the family and see if he's left.

H: We don't even know the number, do we?

M: We could look it up—there can't be too many Evanses in the book. (Actually, I had already looked it up. There were six, most of whom could be eliminated by unlikely location.)

H: (big sigh) You're the one who's worried—why don't *you* call?

M: Because they'll think I'm an anxious hovering mother, and it will look better if *you* call.

H: You realize you're making it impossible for me to call by putting all this pressure on me?

M: Can't we handle the issue of John's safety now and deal with our own interaction later?

H: OK, if he isn't here in ten minutes, I'll call.

Within ten minutes John came, apologetic—suddenly, when it had been time to go, friends had asked him for a ride home. We suggested that another time he check ahead, or call us and let us know that he'll be late or, if he'll be violating the legal curfew, drive directly home and one of us would be glad to return his friends to their homes. It is over. We are shaken, but safe.

There are other dramas of family strain—"I really wish you wouldn't wear dungarees to Aunt Sarah's wedding," or "We're having company for the weekend, will you please clean your room?" or, in a far more serious vein, "I know it's a different time but pre-marital sex still seems like such an emotional risk to me." Families with teen-aged children know them all, and for the children and the adults these episodes that dramatize realignments of loyalty and value from "My parents are mostly in charge" to "*I* am mostly in charge" and the reciprocal diminishment of parental power can be times of strain as well as delight. The old image of "the cozy family" so nicely symbolized in our scene in the motel in Maine may seem at times to reflect an era that is long gone.

It *is* long gone, that time when as parents we were all-powerful and beyond criticism, and there are certainly good things about being free of that, too. (We knew that our pedestal was very shaky and sometimes uncomfortable and it is rather nice to have some time and energy to ourselves again and not to be wondering whether in the sudden quiet someone is pouring glue on the piano keys or whether we are going to have to be up all night with a sick child.) So, we enter a new country as middle-aged parents, and it has its own marvels and hazards.

The marvels are easy to talk about, and we do, unashamedly, writing them in our Christmas letters and our college alumnae magazines and bragging to our friends who, if we will give them equal time, will still be our friends. The accomplishments of our children do become truly impressive. They get glider pilot's licenses and become National Merit scholars and conduct original scientific research and are chosen to sing in a statewide madrigal competition. We are proud. They know things we do not know: they talk about force fields and absolute zero and land use management and cognitive dissonance and they understand the use of symbolism in Faulkner and they compose songs and they are asked to hang their photographs in galleries and to present papers at professional gatherings and they become editors of school papers and they sell sculptures to an art dealer and they get part-time jobs that use their incipient professional skills and they climb in wildernesses we would not tackle and we know they are strong and brave. And with all that, they are developing into young men and women of physical attractiveness and competence and they are, for the most part, compassionate and loving persons, deeply caring, responsible, fun to be with. Sometimes, looking at them and reflecting on our common and individual pasts and how far we have all come together, we wonder—How could it be? How could we be so fortunate? How could they be so fine? Those are the good feelings, and they fill us with gladness.

There are difficult feelings, too, and sometimes it is they that seem to exact a daily nagging cost and we may wonder why, when our lives are so full, we have these feelings of impatience and uneasiness as often as we do.

Some of the difficulty we may feel in our relationships with our teen-agers is due just to the friction sparks of growing up. It is the process here that is important: the ideology is incidental. Does it really matter at all about clothing and the length of hair? In the long run, will it matter whether their rooms looked like the aftermath of a tornado? A mother I knew told of how her daughter, under the guise of weight control, fixed all her meals for herself, ate by herself, at a slightly different time from the rest of the family. This is hard to take, the whole symbolism of food being so important, but it will surely pass, just as most people discover after some experimentation with disorder that it is more pleasant to live in rooms that are moderately orderly and clean. And if—an unlikely prospect—styles in clothing were to change so radically that blue jeans became accepted attire for all occasions—well, there would probably be as many good things as bad to be said for that·and, anyway, we could still put on our silks, laces, tweeds, and mohair and strut around for each other, and for ourselves.

These friction sparks of growing up do not augur permanent unsettling change, but they may still be difficult—which is probably just what they need to be, if our own development and that of our adolescent children are to proceed. A function of these years is to provide an arena for that struggle. Someone has said, in regard to parents and their teen-aged children: "Your need is to need them; their need is not to need you." And even though, as parents, we realize that this is so, and try to make all kinds of allowances for it, and to give our children all kinds of permission to go their own way, to "rebel," and ourselves permission to feel displaced and at the same time encouraging ourselves and each other to move on out to new things now that our parenting is diminishing—still, it is hard, and there is some grinding of gears. In an ideal world, one wonders, would a young person flow naturally from lesser to greater responsibility, and would parents flow naturally from lesser to greater degrees of relinquishment of power? Perhaps. Perhaps not. Some psychologists suggest that conflict and struggle over these shifts of power and responsibility are not just incidental to the agenda of changing roles and degrees of independence—so that somehow if we were wise enough to "do it right" we could accomplish the shifts without pain—but that they are part of the agenda itself: part of the way individuality and independence are perceived and received is by struggle against barriers, against structures that limit. So the problem for parents becomes for us to convey this to our children, knowing even as we do that for their own health they will have to struggle and negotiate with us and be, in some sense, displeased. (If they do not tell us our limits are unacceptable we may hazard a guess that it is so nonetheless and that in ways they consider risky-but-safe they are testing our limits on the side.)

We need to be honest about these limits, too. A child whose parents have loaded him or her with a lot of responsibility will certainly know something is unreal if suddenly the parent backs up and becomes more restraining, so that when the rebellion comes it will still be within acceptable limits. This will not do, and we know it, and so do the children.

Nor will a stance of "let me help you rebel against me" do too well, either. It is hard for us, eager to stay in contact with our children, empathetic with their needs, not to be over-solicitious about their needs to defy us, or to try to adapt our style to theirs to a degree that is not really compatible with our own integrity, and therefore to frustrate the whole thing. They will just have to go farther, until they hit a barrier whose tumbling we cannot tolerate, and have a try at that. I am reminded of the cartoon of the very "with it" parents, long-haired, dungaree-clad, seated cross-legged on the floor in the midst of a psychedelic room and viewing their business-suit-clad youngster outside the door, saying to one another, "Where did we go wrong?" Our children may need, for awhile or perhaps for a long time, to turn away from the institutions in which we have seen our values reflected. How many ministers' children have left the church, at least for awhile? Or children of public officials got into minor scrapes with the law?

There is no way around this stage of mutual struggle, only through it. A social worker I know who works with many families at mid-life says, "The families I feel sorry for are those where the teen-agers never do establish themselves as independent persons—then they have to do it in their twenties, or thirties, or they may even remain overdependent all their lives." This is difficult terrain, and it is often accompanied by anger and hurt feelings and self-reproach, both on the part of parents and of children. The fortunate families are where this process of change and growth is recognized, where it can be talked about, and where there is a lot of mutual respect and love and good humor.

There are other areas of shifting values that are related not only to the inevitable process of growing up, but that also represent real cultural change. We need to understand what aspects of these changes invite us all to growth and expansion of our experience and understanding, and what aspects are the other thing—the struggle for independence.

We have learned much from our own children, some of it easily, some with a good deal of inner and outer foot-dragging. The anthropologist Margaret Mead suggests that this is the first generation where the flow of education goes not only from parent to child, as it has heretofore, but also from child to parent. There are ways, of course, in which parents have always learned from children, as children have developed fields of expertise that are their own and have shared some of that with parents. I think of how our lives are enriched by Peter's knowledge of birds, their flight patterns and locales, and of the aerodynamics of flight. I, too, watch now to see when the birds are gliding on air currents and when they are moving their wings up and down to keep aloft and moving. I think of John's knowledge of cities and how, approaching a downtown area, I now watch for the old houses which were, in the city's youth, built close to the bodies of water and now in their semi-decrepitude still cling to the sides of hills. I think of Steve taking us to the site of a geology field trip and showing us the fossils in the hard rock layers and scooping out clay from the clay layers for us to fashion small sculptures in our hands. I think of Mary's interest and knowledge in psychic phenomena and how that has helped me to pay attention to my unconscious and to feel her companionship and help in some of the mystic experiences that have added new dimensions and meanings to my life. Some of these things I had interest in and some knowledge of before, some I did not; and my life has been greatly enriched by the new material and insight which our children have added out of their own accumulating store to ours.

These extensions of understanding have been easy. There have been others that are not so easy, though nonetheless valuable. There is, I suppose, no area in human experience more loaded with difficulty and delight than that of sexuality, and sexuality has become an endlessly reverberating focus for the sometimes differing perceptions of young people and adults. Here, too, we have learned from our children. I do not want to idealize the young, who certainly have their problems with identity, or to be prejudicial to myself or my generation, who have wended our own way with a mix of success and failure. I do want to acknowledge that life is vastly different now than it was twenty years ago. The advent of reliable contraceptives has extended the options for living together in profound ways. And choices now are made not so much on biological likelihoods—though they, in terms of pregnancy and the possibility of venereal disease still need to be considered—but on the far more complex and demanding bases of the qualities of relationships.

So now that we are virtually freed from the consequences of sex being the likelihood of pregnancy we have a whole new range of consequences to think about, and of precautions in contemplating sex, too. What degree of emotional intimacy is necessary for sex to be good? Do we need marriage for our own security apart from providing security for children? When trouble comes will we need marriage to make us try harder? Is a relationship which needs legal pressures upon it to hold it together worth holding together? To what degree is greater sexual freedom enriching, and where does it begin to fragment us?

It is a Pandora's box, this new freedom, and there may be times when we wish we could slam down the lid and we wish that technology had never brought us to this place. We strain our imaginations to perceive what it must be like growing up today when the answers to the questions may turn out to be the same as ours—and they may not—but they will surely be given for at least somewhat different reasons.

What can we do about all of this—we who want life for our children and more options for them, and who may on the other hand be a bit envious of their freedom to be, as they seem to us to be, more open and honest with one another than we remember ourselves as being when we were, say, sixteen years old? We can be grateful for that freedom, both for them and for all who can make wise use of it. If we begin to be envious of them, let us remember, too, that more choices mean more responsibility, more agonizing. One does not have to look far to see the tremendous pressures the young are put under—for early sex experience, for incorporating other people on an intimate level into your life when you scarcely know yet who you are yourself. We read magazine articles trying to reassure young girls that it is not a disgrace to be a virgin, and there are now counter-attempts in colleges to support men who feel somehow inadequate if they have not had sex experience by the time they are twenty. It may be a freer time, but it certainly is not easier.

We can, as parents, listen to our children, encourage them to talk with us, and be grateful if they do—it says something about their trust in us. We can tell them how we feel about our own sexual choices and how the options look to us from where we stand, and if they occasionally smile wryly at what seems to them our naîveté, our "old-fashioned" ways, that's all right, too. They will make their own choices—all we can do is tell them who we are. Someone said to me once, in talking about one of my sons and the various "what ifs?" of his future: "I assume that if he told you he was going to live with someone you would try to change his mind?" And to my listener's horror I said, "No, I wouldn't. I would try to tell him what my feelings about it were and to say what I thought the hazards of such a choice were, but it's his decision, and it's not my place to appropriate that for him."

I was pleased with myself in that exchange—the son in question was twenty years old—but I have not always been so sure what the right course was. When, and to what degree, do we relinquish control over our children's lives? Chances are that when we are still asking the question, the answer is already in: sooner than you think. By the time young people are fifteen or sixteen they are certainly making their important life decisions on their own. If we are consulted, we are lucky, and can take some pride in the fact that we must have done something right, to still be consulted. But we are consulted as advisors, as sounding boards or, sometimes, we are informed only—a way of sharing—but we are not viewed as persons whose right it is to decide. We do not always accept this, or take it gracefully, or make the right response, but if our relationship with our children has been good, there is a lot of reserve on which to draw, a lot of resilience, and we can be grateful that even in our ineptitudes we are in contact with one another.

Even here, or maybe especially here, there come times when somehow love, trust, unfamiliar terrain, and past history all converge and parents are left with feelings of immense gratitude, when the "chickens come home to roost" and they are good. I remember my son saying to me after he had told me of some new development in his life with which I was not entirely happy and I had expressed to him some of those "where did I go wrong?" feelings probably familiar to most parents, "On the contrary, if you had not made me a loving person . . ." and I thought, Yes, it is a gift, to be a loving person, and we have helped him to be that. Or the time when our daughter had said, after some heavy discussion, "If you want to express your anger and upset feelings to me, I'll be glad to listen," or another time, when I was expressing to her my chagrin at some of the feelings I had in some intense family matter, "You don't have to give reasons for your feelings. It's OK just to have the feelings."

We do learn from our children, find affirmation from them, as when out of regard they tell us, or do not tell us—and it can be either one—what is going on with them. And when our children's friends come to us and say, "This is where I feel at home," or outsiders say of our family, "I can see how close you are" or "Your children have had such freedom to develop their own interests," or the advisor to the youth group in the town we have just moved to says, "They're unusually mature. I was very impressed with them," or "I've never seen a brother and sister care so much about each other," then we breathe a huge inner sigh and think, we have certainly not done it all right, but they are marvelous people. And then, ruefully we wonder, How on earth did that happen? and, more wryly yet, Now why did I worry so much?

We are proud of them and find—a splendid unexpected revelation—that they are proud of us, too! My daughter says, "Is it OK if I take the poem you wrote to show my English teacher?" Or our son says, in contemplating our coming visit to his college campus, "It's not only that I'll be glad to see you, but I want my friends to see my family." Some friends of our oldest son's, just out of college, come to visit and they get to talking with me about writing and with my husband about the meaning of rituals and they are not just being polite—they are really interested! And our children sit with a trace of what Stephen used to call "a proud mother smile" on their faces. Somehow we have come full circle from those early days when our interdependence with our children was nearly complete and they thought we were gods, through years when the cords of our connections with one another have been tested and strained and flailed about and come back together again but in a different way, and we find that, yes, of course we are still parents and children but there are also times when we are incredibly close and cherished friends.

I think of how, in the aftermath of our daughter's death, our sons have helped us, not only with their affection, presence, and the sharing of our common grief, but with insights to bring us light in darkness, a quiet steadiness in a time of emotional havoc. I think of Peter, standing with me in a cold rain outside a gas station on the night she had died. We had come from the hospital, come from the funeral director's where we had had our brief viewing of her body, and now we were waiting while Hoyt made yet another phone call, and we all awaited the arrival of a car we could use to take us back to the vacation compound where we were staying. I had said to Peter, in a kind of dazed incredulity, "You think of the worst thing that could happen to you, and it does and somehow we are still alive, we survive," and he had said, "I've wondered what we would do if one of us died," and then, after some moments, "It'll take time, but we'll feel good again," and I remember my thought, my grateful and unbelieving thought, Could it be? Maybe you are right. If you can say that, maybe it is so.

I think of John, two days later, as we gathered in the living room of our cottage to hold our simple family memorial service, recalling for us some words he had heard at a Quaker meeting for worship when someone, in describing a revered friend, had said, "He left himself unprotected, so that he could be changed," and how John went on to say of Mary how open she was, more than anyone he had known—open to change, and somehow that seemed not only to affirm her, but to begin to give some meaning even to her death—that this change which had come to her, so terrible for us, would indeed lead her into some greater life.

I think of Stephen several nights later, on the eve of our departure from this place to which we had come in expectation and joy and which we were now to leave, and of how for a few minutes in the back room of our cottage I was sharing with him my feeling of being overcome with grief and all the what-if feelings that come in the aftermath of accidental death: what if she had been wearing different shoes? what if the terrain on which she fell had been soft instead of rocky? what if she could have clung to the horse's back another thirty seconds until someone had been able to reach her? And slowly, haltingly, he had said how there is no end to the way you can torture yourself that way and always after a thing has happened you can see how you could have avoided it, but you never can, before, and the only alternative to doing things that might not turn out well would be to do nothing and that would not be like Mary and I said, no, it wouldn't, no. He said he had been thinking a lot the last few days and watching the creatures of the mountain, the chipmunks, the birds, the little bugs and how some of those bugs lived a summer only or a few weeks and that was their whole life and it was a good life for them. It was the same with Mary, he said, she had had her life, her *Now*, and it was rich and good, and I said, yes, yes, tears of grief and gratitude pouring down my face. He went on to say how *our Now* is what we have, too, and of course we expected more for her, and of course we remember and we look ahead and we are sad. But our Now is what we have, this moment is our life, and it isn't bound or ruined by those sadnesses and memories. Hearing him, I recalled the last lines of a poem by Howard Nemerov that has long been a favorite of mine and I quoted that to him, "And the mind of God, the flash across the gap of being, thinks in the instant absence of forever: now," and he said, "Yes, that's it," and after awhile we dried our tears and went into the living room where the others were gathered for our last night visit together. I don't know what there was in all of that to bring a glimmer of peace and hope to me, only that I felt a great weight begin to lift, and

I felt that I had passed out of some kind of water shed. I knew there would be many other valleys of despair. But from this one, on this evening, I had been lifted out, by the wisdom, the love, the ministry, of my son.

Hoyt and I think of our relationships with our own parents during the years after our growing up, and I see in that model some of the ranges of possibilities for our children and ourselves. I speculate about the "areas of overlap" we have had with our parents, where our interests and values are common enough that we can talk about them freely and share them with each other. I think of the places where the language of our lives is different and there probably is not a whole lot of common ground. I recall the times when we have tried to share something important with our parents and it has ended in dismay; I think of other times when we have taken risks, hoping to bridge that "other generation gap" between middle-aged parents and their parents, and we have been rewarded by a leap of understanding from them far beyond what we had hoped for, and what an occasion for gratitude and wholeness that has been. I suppose both kinds of experiences will be present in our lives with our children. We have stayed close with our parents—visited back and forth, had family reunions in the summers. I hope for that. I hope for, and expect, mutual trust and respect, that we shall continue to care about each other. I recall a young psychologist saying to me once, "My father is sixty-five and he's starting therapy and he wants to tell me about it." I recall the vicarious pang I felt for his father and my unspoken question was, "And do you want to hear it?" I hope we always "want to hear it" about each other.

There is a way, of course, in which we do not believe any of it. Crossing the country, seeing colts and mares, seeing baby pigs scuttling after their mothers, seeing mother birds spending their life energy in the hatching and feeding of their young, I see myself—there you are, I say, and only secondarily do I remember, No, not anymore. My mother thinks I am a young woman. "You're only young once," she says, urging me to buy a bright plaid coat. "If *you* are middle-aged," she says to me, half scoffing and half in disbelief, "what does that make me?" A friend says, "I am forty-five and I don't feel all that mature and stable, all that different from when I was sixteen." We hear the words of the song from "Fiddler on the Roof": "I don't remember getting ol-der . . . When—did—they?" We receive invitations and schedules in the mail for our son's graduation from college. From *college!* How could it be? But it is, and we go to the graduation weekend and we sit in the auditorium at the baccalaureate service and the Roman Catholic priest in his sermon to the graduates says, "May you always be young, and may your youth always bring you joy," and I think, yes—that's good. I feel young still, and full of joy, a sometimes bittersweet joy, but joy nonetheless. Then the choir sings "How Lovely Is Thy Dwelling Place" and I remember myself singing that song in my college choir—could it have been that long ago? How quickly time passes. I look over at my husband and see there are tears in his eyes.

Months later, we go down to see the apartment which our son and his love have cleaned, painted, and arranged with their belongings and now they want us to come and see it. It is lovely and familiar—high-ceilinged old rooms, light from the high windows, walls in mid-repair—they are still working on it. In the kitchen is an old-fashioned refrigerator that vibrates so strongly as to give the person sitting in the nearest kitchen chair a gratuitous body massage. In the living room a coverlet is spread to cover the holes in an old but comfortable sofa that "goes with the apartment."

I look at my son. Has it been that long? I am in my apartment in Lansdowne, my residence when I had my first job out of college. I see the flame-colored drapes I made for the window in the corner, the blue semi-gloss paint on the kitchen wall, the table we pulled out from the living room wall for dinners when company came. One of our frequent guests was the man who stands beside me now, my husband of nearly twenty-five years. And now the children of our marriage are grown. What shall we be to each other in the future? What do we hope for as we look toward our relationship with our children in the years ahead?

Thinking of that question, I remember one vacation when the boys had decided to climb Estes Cone—one of the lesser peaks in the area of the Rocky Mountains where we were staying. They wanted to climb it for the trip itself, and as an acclimatization for more ambitious climbs they planned to make later on. They would start early in the morning, they told us, in order to reach the top and be back off the mountain before afternoon thunderstorms might come and make it unsafe. They wanted to signal us, they said, from the top of the mountain. They had a pair of signal mirrors of polished metal. They would take one with them, and leave the other one with us. They showed us how you must catch the rays of the sun on the mirror and then by means of a small pinhole in the mirror's surface, line up and redirect that light to the spot to which you are signaling. The mirrors were Peter's and he instructed both his father and me, "You may have to get yourself at a weird angle," he said, "to catch the light and send it back to us." We nodded, yes, we thought we understood how it worked. "Be in the parking lot, at 11:30," Peter said, "and if we have reached the top of the Cone, we'll signal to you, and you can signal back."

The next morning when we got up they had, as planned, already gone and as 11:20 came we went to the parking lot, the mirror in our hands, to watch the top of Estes Cone, and to wait. There were three generations of us, waiting—Mary was with us, Hoyt's mother and father, and Hoyt and I—five of us, altogether. Hoyt and I experimented a little with the mirror— Peter was right, it was difficult to catch the sun's light and send it back to the mountaintop at this time of day. We agreed that I, being of the two of us the more adept with my hands, would hold the mirror. As 11:30 approached the suspense grew, we all riveted our eyes to the top of the mountain and waited. "They should be there," Hoyt said. It was 11:29. Then, exactly on the dot of 11:30 the first silver flash came from the high peak of the mountain. They had arrived! "There they are!" we shouted. Quickly now, with the mirror. I moved it to the angle I had practiced, the way I thought it was going to work. But the beam shot off to the side. I shifted the mirror, angled it, moved it down toward the ground, while we all held our breath and the consternation grew, but I could not get it right. "Here," I said in a panic, and passed the mirror to Hoyt. He took the mirror from me and dropping to the ground he lay on his back and caught the beam of the sun's light and angled the metal plate in line with the tiny hole. "I've got it!" he cried and the beam went back to the top of Estes Cone, right to the spot

53

where the boys were flashing their beam to us, now in staccato flashes. "Hurray!" we all shouted, and the silver flash came back, down the steep angle of the mountain and across the valley to us—Flash! Flash!—and our cheer continued and people on the porch of the lodge looked at us but we did not care.

A cloud came over the top of Estes Cone then, and the signaling stopped. We put the mirror back in our pocket and moved away from the parking lot. They would be coming down now, and would tell us how it was. When I think of the changing varieties of parenthood and wonder what the years ahead will be for us, I think of that time on Estes Cone when our children, grown to adulthood, went on their own distant adventure up that mountain, and how they wanted us to know about it when they got there, and we waited and sent back our flash, and then how the boys came back down and we told how it was for each of us, how it all worked, and how good it was to be together again in the joy and presence of each other. That is how I hope it will always be.

4

The Shadow of the Mountain: Seeing the Limits of Life

"The noon of life," writes C. G. Jung, "is the moment of greatest deployment, when a man is devoted entirely to his work, with all his ability and all his will. But it is also the moment when the twilight is born: the second half of life is beginning. . . . At midday the descent begins, determining a reversal of all the values and ideals of the morning."

Reading this, do we recognize it as true? Do we start to protest—wait a minute, it's not like that, it's not a descent. Maybe, we may say, it's an ascent but in different terms. But even in our protestations there is something in the words of Jung we recognize as true, though we would just as soon not be reminded of it.

Perhaps, rather than Jung's figure of the descent of the mountain, we prefer that of Oliver Wendell Holmes in "The Chambered Nautilus," in which the animal builds for itself a successively larger and larger shell until, released at last, it leaves its shell altogether. Or in a more droll and understated fashion, we may see ourselves in one of the cartoons from *The New Yorker*, in which two middle-aged women are seated on a sofa, looking toward the window, where the husband of one of them stands looking soberly out into space. The wife says, "He used to regard the human comedy with amused tolerance, until one day he realized it included him."

In whatever terms it comes to us, the middle of life has difficult shoals and we can come through these times either reborn or in a continuing lowgrade depression that leaves us functioning but without much joy and purpose in our lives. Sometimes, we may move back and forth between these moods.

Middle life has been described as a time when we come to see the limits of life. And we do.

Our bodies continue to lose ground in the fight for youth and beauty. It is easier to put on weight, the doctor starts including an electrocardiogram, especially if we are men, in our annual physical exam. We take to wearing turtleneck shirts and neck scarves to camouflage our drooping neck tissue, we watch for cholesterol counts and realize it is better to let somebody else shovel the heavy snow. We wonder whether our sexual potency and appetite will last as long as we do. In a newspaper article a few years ago on one of New York's high fashion stores was a picture of a back room where cloth and wire mannequins of regular customers were kept and it described how, over the years, the store personnel would adapt each mannequin to its owner's body shape, winding strips of cloth around the center body as "waistlines thicken." We resent youth worship and "agism" and we resolve to be proud of ourselves when we are no longer young, but for aesthetic, health, and self-image reasons we, too, try to preserve ourselves. We go to exercise classes, we may join Weight Watchers and health spas, we become more careful about what we eat and drink—though I hope we are choosy about which advertising lures we succumb to. (One health food store near us advertised "tiger milk" with all kinds of inferences about its youth-restoring qualities and one could only wonder, along with some speculations about the qualities of tigers—how did the procurers of tiger milk manage to get it?) We take up meditation partly for its religious value and partly to quiet our nerves and reduce our blood pressure—and we are right in thinking that these are related to each other. We wonder about biofeedback and about promises of new research that in a few more decades science will be able to prolong the vigor of middle life into old age and extend productive life by many years. We know that will be too late for us and there are days when we are sorry and other days when we do not care— would it not upset the delicate balance of our psyches, this late in life, to have to reform our expectations to include an additional twenty or thirty years of living? "I don't want to live longer than eighty-five," says the father in Joseph Heller's novel, *Something Happened*, "and I don't want to die sooner than a hundred and eighty-six."

Our minds continue to operate now at high efficiency, but once in a while when it takes us a few seconds longer to remember the name of an acquaintance, or of a city we stayed in on our way to our last year's vacation, we see that the mind, too, is less elastic, the energy moves more slowly through the brain and we hope that we make up in wisdom what we lack in speed.

We see our potential limits in ways other than the slow lessening of our body's power. Our career expectations may of necessity become more modest or we may continue to grapple with unfulfilled ambition. We may be slow to acknowledge that others are successful in a way we are not. I don't remember when it was—ten years ago, maybe, or fifteen?—when I finally accepted the fact that the greater achievement of others in areas where I, too, had some knowledge and skill was no longer a function of their either being older than I or their being precocious achievers. At twenty-five, one can view the achievements of contemporaries, though perhaps jealously, as something of a fluke. Like the fellow-student in graduate school who, not yet thirty, was feeling anxious about his achievements and, the Cuban revolution then being much in the news, exclaimed in only half-jest, "Look at Castro—he's my age and he's already got a country!" At forty, one can no longer think of strikingly successful contemporaries as precocious. If we have not "made it" now, will we ever?

If we are in the arts our illusions may sustain us later into middle life. If we used, in our youth, to identify with the romantic artists—Keats, Mozart, who flared into an early artistic creativity and then died young—we now turn to Grandma Moses as our hope-inducing model, or at least to James

Michener, who published his first work after the age of forty. There can always be, we say to ourselves, marvelous success in the next work—though even here we suspect we are whistling in the dark—even in art there are very few like Grandma Moses.

We see the limitations of our power to have much of anything more to do with the formation of our children's lives. For good or ill, we have done our work as nurturing parents. There will be other forces that continue to affect their development as young adults, but we are largely spectators and, if we are fortunate, sharers in the results of that, but our role as agents in their growth is certainly minimal. Our children do leave us, physically and emotionally, to strike out on their own and while they may come back as friends—and, yes, as children, now grown and independent—we certainly do not have the power to affect their lives that we once had.

We see, by middle life, that our power to control social and personal trouble is limited. Try as we may, we cannot restore justice to society in any overall sense. We cannot see the end to problems of world hunger, poor prison systems, or social structures that grind down dignity and initiative. Never, really, had we thought it could all be done, but the mood becomes more sober and, if we are not careful, almost resigned, by the time we reach middle life and have belonged to fifteen task forces and written many letters to our congressional representatives and campaigned for twenty office seekers. We know that for the most part social progress is eked out slowly, a paragraph at a time, and while change can be of infinite value to a person who could not get food stamps and now, because of the change in a clause of the law, can get them, still, our hopes for wide-scale improvement in social conditions are often quite subdued.

We are equally powerless, and often more devastated—the intensity of our personal connections being what they are—to control events of personal disaster and trouble. Sickness strikes us down, people our age begin to have heart attacks, sudden terrible accidents befall someone in our family, and we are powerless. We see the limits of life when tragedy strikes us and we can do . . . nothing.

We see that we do not have endless opportunity for "fixing

things up" in those many areas of life that are left to us. It is a commonly acknowledged phenomenon of middle life that old problems we did not solve in our adolescence return to us in our "middlescence" and renew their demands for resolution. And we feel the urgency of that: if we have trouble with human relationships and have assumed things would get better with time—well, there isn't an infinite amount of time left for those improvements to occur "in the natural course of events." We may find ourselves seeking out counseling to help with a process we had previously assumed would, given enough time, take care of itself. Our marriages come up for new scrutiny. There are, I am told, more divorces in the decade of the 40s than in any other, as couples get a panicky "last chance at happiness" feeling, or find that, with the children gone, there is little to hold them to one another any more.

We must learn to live with ineradicable mistakes—not everything *can* be "fixed up," even if there were time. So we must come to terms with our own guilt—the mistakes we made that we cannot undo—our regrets at not having been better parents when our children were small, the memory of times when we hurt someone else we cared about and we cannot retrieve that—it is done. Can we forgive ourselves for those past mistakes, now that we "know better" but know there is no way our present wisdom and sensitivity can swing back over time and right an old wrong? As our parents grow old and frail we are sometimes acutely aware of their needs of us, but also of our spouse's needs, and our children's, our friends' and, yes, of our own—can we accept the fact that we are not perfectly adequate to all situations and having done the best that we can, be content with that?

Time itself begins to close in on us—not now, not right away, but we see the handwriting on the wall. We have watched, often in retrospect, opportunities go by us and thought, Well, I missed that one, but I'll catch the next one that comes around, whether it is a trip we might have taken, a relationship we might have cultivated, a gift we might have given to ourselves or someone else—even an impromptu speech we might have made at a community gathering. But by middle life we can sense the limits of those occasions, too. A friend said to me recently, "I'm going to North Carolina to help my mother celebrate her 75th birthday. I don't have the time. I don't have the money. But I'm going." I have thought often, and with gratitude, of my husband's insistence, during our children's growing years, that we spend money we could sometimes ill afford on family vacation trips. My impulse was always to "wait, we can't afford it." "The years will be gone," he would say, "and then we won't be able to have them with us." I have been grateful to him many times for that urging and now, even I would know that one does not wait to capture important human experiences until all the conditions are right—by then, if such a time ever comes, the people with whom to share them may be gone. At mid-life we know in our psyches what reason has told us all along—time will run out on us, even on us.

There is a quotation from Paul Tillich that comes to mind: "Time is our destiny. Time is our hope. Time is our despair. And time is the mirror in which we see eternity." We sense time as all these things as, halfway through the normal span of years we speculate about the end of life and what we shall have time yet to do and knowing that is a question to which none of us has the answer we begin, nevertheless, to value our time with new urgency. For twenty years I have told myself, Some day I'm going to learn to play the cello. I am beginning to realize I had better start soon or else dismantle my fantasy. Petty interruptions to our days may annoy us more than they used to. Recently I had to call a plumber and before the job was done right, he had had to make three return calls to our house, which ate heavily into the time I had counted on for my work. I minded terribly, though the plumber and I parted on the best of terms. Years ago, it wouldn't have mattered so much—I could always do my work "later." But now, it is not only the question of publisher's deadlines to meet, it is also my sense that, symbolically anyway, there is not that much time to spare any more, and if I lose my work time now I will not have it back again.

The spectre of aging . . . I ask my son, as I contemplate the whole subject of middle life, "Does middle age seem like something you dread?" and he says, "No. Old age seems more scary." The neighbors grow old. Our parents' contemporaries seem suddenly frail. Visiting my mother in the hospital in one of the several illnesses of her late years, I pass in the corridor a row of wheelchairs in which three old women sit against the wall. They are thin and gaunt. The hair of each of them is brushed back and caught in a pony tail at the back of her head. Their eyes are bright and dart about to look at each motion that takes place in the room before them. But there is no knowledge in their eyes. The face of the most alert wears a constant eager smile. Each time I pass her I smile and nod and say hello. Her eager gratitude stabs me—she is so grateful for so little. My mother is physically frail and there are times when her memory for a sought-after detail does not work for her. She looks at me, wondering. "I can't remember," she says, puzzled and dismayed. There are other times when she mobilizes the full intelligence and sensitivity that have been hers and we talk together in ways that are enriching and lift our hearts because we have grief and speculation to contend with and we need one another. As I go by these women in the hall with their eager vacant eyes I think, I hope my mother does not get that way, and then, a speculation I can hardly fathom and yet it comes to me as an incredible possibility, What about me? As I talk with my children and my husband after the death of my father we wonder together what our responsibilities and possibilities are now in the continuing care of my mother. There is present another shadow, standing behind the figure of my mother in her age and dependence and her frailty and the considerable resources she can muster, and that shadowèd figure is I—What about me? These young people, my children, are, in thirty years, the middle-aged children, sitting around a table, trying to figure out what to do about their aging parents. My husband's family has a history, on one side, of great longevity. I hope it lasts. I do not expect to die soon, though at periods in my life an early death has been a compelling fantasy. But of course I do not know. The spectre of aging . . . What about me? Will I be helpless and weak? Will I be difficult? Will my mind stay keen? Will it hurt me—growing old? Theodore Roethke writes in his notebook, "Me, I don't want to die. I want to live to a long self-indulgent happy productive dumb old age." The spectre of aging—shall we be able to cope?

The spectre of death . . . Old school teachers die. Our parents die—How could they! They must be the exception to the rule.

The Growing Season

How could they die? Who will take care of us? The death of one's parents means many things to their middle-aged children: grief at losing not only our parents but all the association we have shared with them; a certain relief for them, if they have been sick or very old and frail and life has seemed a burden to them; a relief, for ourselves, if we have been preoccupied with their health and their care; a final loss of childhood, which has, of course, been long gone. The song fragment comes to me, "Into your arms I'd fly, Safe in your arms I'd be." It is the image of my mother, that figure whose protecting arms are the ultimate haven of children. It has been many, many years since I have run to my mother for comfort and security. And yet somewhere in the back of the mind the image persists. If my mother dies, who will take care of me? I will, of course. My husband will, my children and friends—we will all care for each other, as we have been doing for a long time. And yet to have one's parents die is to lose a symbolic "help in time of trouble" that no one can replace.

The death of parents may also mean the dissolution of an old homestead, if our parents have lived in the family home in their old age. Then the task becomes ours—the physical and emotional labor of sorting over all the things. What shall we save and what shall we throw away—the necessary separating of the person's memory from the person's *things*. If I throw away my father's treasured school photos, am I being unkind to his memory? Would he mind? The pictures of my mother and her mother, posed with some cousins on the lawn of an English vicarage—will these people's lives be extended if I keep the photograph, or diminished if I throw it away? Irrational considerations, but they rise out of the depths of old trunks and come from the backs of old closets to ask their primal questions of us, and to make eyebrow-raising, speculative faces at our accumulations of *our* mementoes, and to remind us of our own mortality. For one of the things the death of parents says to us is, you're next. I remember, after my grandfather died, going over in my head how many more death experiences in my family I would have to endure before it would be my turn. The count was strictly chronological—one for my one remaining grandparent, one apiece for each of my parents, one for my older sister. My younger brother and sister would, of course, die after I did. I have since learned that chronology is not the sole determiner of death, but it is also true that as we get older the advance guards that stand between us and death fall away. Now we are "the older generation," and death is no longer an alien possibility, somewhere on the other side of the globe. It could be in the next county only, or just across the road.

Aging . . . retirement . . . death—inconceivable events? Strangers that suddenly come to live with us? My husband says, "When I was twenty, and had possibly fifty or sixty more years—I couldn't imagine that. I had no experience into which to put that knowledge." Now that he's getting close to fifty . . . he goes on to say that, unless he's unusual, he won't live that long again. So, he can imagine the rest of his career, the end of his life. There is this now or never quality because he can see the limits. It is the inevitability of time—at first, years ago, it was a cloud no bigger than a man's hand. In middle life it gets bigger and bigger.

What does it all mean? I can work as long as I want to, so the symbol of retirement is different for me. But my husband will retire, at least partially, assuming he lives past the age of seventy, now mandatory retirement age for United Methodist ministers. At annual conference—a gathering of ministers and representative laypersons of our denomination—each year one of the highlights is the retirement service. I have been to a number of these occasions now, and am always torn between the poignancy of the moment and my fervent wish that something will prevent me from being a principal in such an emotionally demanding experience, when the retiring ministers and their spouses stand and are offered the opportunity to "say a few words." The speeches are often a rich blend of pathos, of gratitude, of obviously diminished physical power, and an occasional humorous event. One retiree, at a time when pastoral placements were officially a closely guarded secret until they were ceremonially intoned at the conference's closing session, announced his own upcoming part-time appointment—bringing first gasps and then a kind of startled, glad laughter from the assembled congregation.

At last year's service, one of the men, after thanking God and the United Methodist Church for the opportunities that had been his, for health to do his work and courage to do it, said, in what seemed to me the understatement of the year, "I have not looked forward to this occasion with any great anticipation." I wonder how it will be for us—my husband and me—if we live that long and participate in this event. It is not imminent. But it is no longer an utter impossibility, either. The "young Turks"—the generation of enthusiastic and initially radical ministers who entered the ministry along with my husband—have graying hair, now. They are no longer the youthful renegades, out to reform the church. They are the statesmen, stateswomen, and their speeches at national gatherings are quoted in the church press and have a tone of more modest reform now, though no less integrity and hope. At the conclusion of the retirement service is "the passing of the mantle." It is one of the stages of the incorporation of the new ministers into the conference. At the appointed time, they stand. How young they look! The name of each is called, and we applaud. It is a holy time and, knowing that we—my husband and I—are at a career stage that is midway between the retirees and the new eager group of the young, I wonder again, How will it be for us?

The last part of the service is a reading of the names of "the honored dead." It is a quiet moment. My father has died during the past year, and reading in the program I make a quick check to see if any have died on the day of my father's death. None has. We stand to sing, "From earth's wide bounds, from ocean's farthest coast, Through gates of pearl streams in the countless host." I did not know any of these persons whose names have been read. It is for my father that I sing, "Alleluia, alleluia." The spectre of death—not for myself. Not yet. But some day—it is no longer the unthinkable stranger.

What do we do with all of this, as we see the limits of power, of life, of time, of relationship, and seeing our limitations, we wonder what to do.

An article in *Psychology Today* on adult life stages speaks of "the urgencies of the early 40s and the mellowing and self-acceptance of the 50s." Someone else has referred to the years of middle life as "the bonus years," a time when our urges for power and peak performance begin to level off and, freed from the responsibilities of parenting and the early urgencies of career drives, we can begin to relax a little, in the realization that life is short and full of uncertainty—let us, therefore, savor and use the time we have.

We may begin to narrow down on those areas of interest and those causes which have been ours. We had a young graduate student visiting us recently, a musicologist, a student of music history. My husband asked him whether he had a particular field of music history which was his specialty. He said, "Oh, no. I'm too young," and went on to say that for awhile he was supposed to keep a generalized competence in the whole range of music history. Later on, it would be appropriate for him to specialize. At the other extreme is the musician whose musical taste became so refined that he was interested only in works for the thirteenth-century Spanish lute. One wonders how old he was before that kind of specialization seemed legitimate to him. Perhaps that is too narrow a range of interest for most of us, and we certainly need to be aware of the dangers of specializing too soon and too narrowly, but there is a sense of relief, too, of appropriateness and a well-earned reprieve in this process of centering on those interests which emerge as our own. I flip through the pages of the several magazines I read regularly and, at last, am quite comfortable at skipping over analyses of the economic situation or alternate suggestions for revising the state constitution. I stop where I want to—at the discussions of literature and the arts, at material on women's roles, at articles on psychology or religion, at sociology if it is presented in personal terms. If the time comes that I need to know more about economics, I'll learn it then. But not now. The things I need, as Harvey Cox says in *Seduction of the Spirit,* "to survive, choose, fight back, grow, learn, keep alive," are engaging enough. It is in a way like the person who upon reaching the age of forty said, "Now I don't have to like tennis any more."

The same is true of the social causes in which we invest ourselves. I was at a meeting not long ago of a group working on a good cause and the subject came up of recruiting more people to help. One of the young women present began bewailing the lack of response to this cause which she had got in her appeal for help at the meeting of another cause. "One of them said to me," she reported, " 'I'm in a political caucus,

The Growing Season

I'm in the League of Women Voters—' " and the woman had gone on to name several other causes in which she had invested herself. "But," my friend had said to her, "can you quit?" The others of us in the room, all a little older, looked at her and at one another and then someone said, "You have to." It is not that one quits, but that one chooses.

It is not always easy to choose. You must choose not only your causes, but the degree to which you get involved in them: will you send money? will you address envelopes? will you make speeches? will you organize a study group? It is those in mid-life who have time for these things, surely more than young parents do. And yet, the will falters, the mind brings back all those other causes in which energy has been mobilized, and the need for choosing sings out loud and clear. A friend of mine, a Roman Catholic priest who has given much of his life energy to promoting good causes, says, in discussing his stage of life—which is slightly older than middle age, "I have gotten off the guilt machine." It is a fine line to walk— somewhere between being fragmented and immobilized by the espousal of too many causes on the one hand and giving up one's responsibility and saying, in effect, social forces are too big for me. Let them roll. Perhaps there comes, by middle life, a kind of perspective that says, I will do what I can. I will leave the rest to others.

If we wondered, years ago, whether we might become president of the company, or hold a distinguished academic chair at a prestigious university and we are, still, an under-secretary of finance or an assistant professor and we see younger men and women passing us in achievement and ac-claim—yes, that is hard. But we make our peace with it and, not just as a "sour grapes" phenomenon but with a wisdom born of time, we realize that high-powered success exacts terrible costs of individuals and families and that, really, the place where we are is a good place to be. A man I know, re-flecting on his own place in a hierarchy in which he is neither at the top nor the bottom, says, "I really have gotten away from the rat race. I might move up another level or two, but beyond that it would be the principle of promoting a person beyond his level of competence. I like what I do. I do it well." I have known this man for a long time. I knew him when the future was wide open, the divergencies in the path were largely un-known, and the pressure of an unfocused ambition coursed through his life. I rejoice to see how, in middle life, he has "come to rest" about his work—savoring it, enjoying it, with hopes and plans for it as well as haggling with its occasional frustrations, but content. He is fortunate to have "found his place," and I know that he has worked hard to do that, and I know there are many who go through their vocational lives without ever having found their place. I realize that part of his ease with vocational life is a confluence of skill and oppor-tunity; part of it is result of the passing of the years.

Our relationships with our children—and this, too, has been our career—certainly take on a different tenor by the time we reach mid-life. Of course there are ways we might wish they were a bit different (they would wish the same for us, too!) But they are responsible for themselves now, to make their own decisions. So, we can leave that all to them, and enjoy them for the people they are. It is not, of course, only responsibility that we release, it is also a lot of time and energy to follow our own interests, even to enjoy our surroundings in the midst of our own degree of clutter and decor.

There is another level at which, by mid-life, we are freed of responsibility. If we had ever thought we were somehow in ultimate control of our lives, by middle life we recognize that this is not so. I am not advocating that we abandon responsi-bility for life direction or quality, only that we recognize that life is full of contingencies over which we have no control and while the contingencies may bring us terrors, they may also bring us a measure of strange freedom. The psychologist Ernest Becker, in a taped interview close to the time of his death from cancer, described his own point of view as needing to take into account all kinds of life terrors from which we usually try to hide. "How suddenly the terrors come" he says, and it is only after we have acknowledged that that we begin to understand our place in the world, and our relationship to God. Becker was asked how that made him feel—the irrational-ity of tragedy in human life, and he said, "I am relieved of the burden of responsibility for my own life," and went on to say how there is a trust beyond accident and death and terror. Not too soon should we give up our sense of jurisdiction over our life and, I suppose, never completely so. But there is a sense in which, by middle life, we have seen enough irrationality, enough occasions where, despite good planning, wisdom, and intention, control of our lives is wrested from us to think, Well, there are events I cannot control. Therefore I will go with them. In that there is also freedom.

Perhaps the freedom of middle life is generalized, all of a piece. Some aspects may be unwelcomed. But some are fine. Did we, at the height of those years of involvement in child-rearing, ever think we would have this many free evenings, this much freedom to decide what to do next? Shall we go to a play on Friday? Shall we stay out until 3 A.M. knowing there are no children at home to worry about, or to reassure that we are safe? Shall we take the weekend and drive into the mountains? or enroll in a seminar at the local college? or invite a friend to dinner without having to check everybody's schedule first? Shall we make some major change in living style that we have contemplated for a long time but have put off?

Do we think we are too old to change? Why? Now is the time when, at least for women who have found their vocation in the raising of children, the slate is almost clear again, and a kind of taking stock and beginning again is possible for us the likes of which we have not seen for twenty years. Just *because* we begin to see that time is short, we need to take the adventurous risk—if not now, when?

It is the quality of time that matters. I heard a psychologist, speaking on relating to the dying, say that those who are terminally ill are very exciting patients with whom to do psychotherapy. "The patient," she said, "usually feels very much alive." I remember my friend whose father began psychotherapy at the age of sixty-five, and I feel vicariously the excitement of it for that man.

Another friend, a man in his early forties, has leukemia and, in a stage of remission now, he tells how at one of the critical moments in his illness, he did not know when he went to sleep whether he would live through the night. "I woke up in the morning," he said, "and I was alive. I had another day." He paused. "It is a great thing," he said, "to have another day." The *quality* of time.

I hope, as we come to middle life, that some of our pretensions to dignity become less necessary and we can come out and play again. Maybe when we were young adults, still proving to ourselves and others that we were grownups and not children, we needed to maintain a level of sober deportment that befits those "on the way up." I certainly do not advocate a perpetual clowning around or any irresponsible foolishness. I do think that one of the freedoms of middle life is to be able with more abandon to express the child in one's self. Eccentricity is the prerogative of those who are no longer young—What have we to lose? I read of an Oxford don, a classical scholar, whose garden wall bordered on a street where, especially on Sundays, there was heavy pedestrian traffic. Each Sunday this learned scholar would climb out on a tree limb that extended over the sidewalk, and bark at the people who passed by on the way to church. I'm sure the man was, as reputed, a fine scholar. I would be willing to wager that he was not young. What young man could be so free?

As a teen-ager I attended many conferences for youth, many of them sponsored by religious groups trying to help us sort out our values, commit ourselves to faith and good works. I remember little of the programmed intellectual or spiritual content of those conferences, though I look upon them as good experiences. But I remember with unflagging delight the philosophy professor from an eastern university who sent us all into paroxysms of laughter and delight by doing a "chicken act"—a bizarre representation of a stalking chicken, with hands folded up into armpits and elbows flapping, with legs in jerky extended strut out in front, and a marvelous ricocheting sound of a chicken crow emerging as he stalked across the stage. I was so taken with the chicken act I have adopted it as my own, and have regaled many audiences of nieces and nephews, my own children, and not a few astonished grownups by my later day rendition. I'm sure that had a young person done the chicken act we would have enjoyed it, but that this middle-aged man, of cherubic face and diffident, scholarly mien, should have cast aside some veneer of dignity and joined us in this canticle to the absurd and lovely foolishness of life—it made us comrades in the human enterprise just as surely as our weightier discussions of love and evil and goodness. As I make my own pilgrimage through middle age, I remember my friend. I remember, too, the suggestion that for Christians the last sound may be one of laughter—that we share in the pain of the world and there are times when our personal sorrow is all we can see. But if God is good and Christ gives us hope, perhaps the last joke is on death and destruction, not on us at all.

There are other ways of giving expression to the child in us that are not so extreme as the chicken-strutting philosophy professor. A friend my age has a splendid collection of dolls. She has become a student of doll history, costume, and a skilled seamstress in creating authentic period and nationality clothing. She also arranges the dolls in family groupings, gives them names, personalities, and spins splendid and involved fantasies about them. Her husband, a physicist by profession, and a lover of beautiful objects, has recently joined in and now has several dolls that are his—miniature dolls in beautiful nationality costumes that sit on his bureau. "These are my dolls," he says, a little abashed, but not much, to have succumbed to the family mania.

My husband cultivates a compost pile. We have more compost on our one-half acre lot than a farmer could use in a truck garden. We have two sections of compost pile, divided by brick walls, and a decorative enclosure of brick work, which our children refer to as "the Chinese wall." If a lovely weed blooms in the compost pile, my husband may dig it out and transplant it to some other spot. He carries tea leaves out, picks up twigs from the yard, and of course, all the grass clippings. What young man, intent upon establishing himself and the basic mechanics of his household, could spend so much time and care on this splendid superfluity of compost? There *are* freedoms that go with being middle-aged.

Is there a "bright side" to the prospect of aging? It is not upon us yet, but we can see its shadow leaning toward us. We look to the people we know who can help us—those who seem to have achieved in their age a serenity, a continuing full participation in life that gives us hope, that seems exciting. I think of our grandmother who at ninety-eight cannot get around very well, but still writes letters to us in a firm round hand, letters full of style and zest and appreciation for new things. A few years ago, when she was more mobile, she was wont to wear outdoors on a cloudy day a gold aluminized raincoat, ordered by her as a mail-order item from a company in which her oldest son was a high official. "I thought," she said, turning to get into a car, "that if anybody should have a gold aluminum raincoat, I should." In a quieter mood, she tells how she keeps an atlas on her reading table. "I like to look at maps at the end of the day," she says, "and I keep my atlas handy, and study it. Or sometimes," she says, looking out the window that faces onto a busy street, "I watch the cars go by, and count the different colors. Then I figure out, say, the proportion of red cars per hundred." She has, like all true parents, an immodest pride in her descendants and a few of them have published books. Some are technical books and she does not understand their contents. "I like to see them anyway," she says. "I like to read the names." She confesses to urging her adult children into controversial discussions. "I read different points of view," she says, naming magazines both to the political right and the political left. "I don't want to get into the discussions myself," she says—"I have such strong feelings and it would get too intense. But I like to hear other people discuss and then I listen. What do you think," she leans forward slightly, "of the supersonic transport?"

Well, this grandmother is both exceptional and fortunate—she is unusually competent and has people she loves who can do for her things she cannot do. She is certainly heartening to be with, and to think about. There are others—a distant cousin, now an old man, shows us his extensive library and record collection. "When I was young," he says, "I couldn't go on to school. So now that I'm retired" (he has been a cattle farmer in the midwest). "I like to listen to music. And I study. I'm learning a lot about geology now," he says, indicating with a sweep of his arm a set of encyclopedias along the wall of his small frame house out here on the prairie. Another pair of cousins, married late in life and each now retired from a university faculty, spend about half of each year making an extended trip with their travel trailer hitched on behind their car, touring one section of the country or another, stopping to camp and to sightsee and to visit their many relatives. The wife has recently taken up a more extensive study of photography, and has had her work exhibited. I read how the writer,

The Growing Season

W.B. Yeats, as an old man, after a life of artistic and political involvement that was often psychically painful, was able to look back on that and to write of "the amenity" of his life—that in retrospect all had "become consecrated" and he was left with a "sense of grateful indebtedness to life." I wonder, Can I? Will I, too, have survived my tragedies and delights with such serenity? I am comforted, even by the possibility.

What if we are not so fortunate? What if we are poor, or sickly, or become so difficult no one wants to be around us? What if we are left alone? These are uninviting prospects. They are also far away, unknowable. Sufficient unto the day is the anxiety thereof. We shall have to do our best to plan for as comfortable an old age as we can manage, for ourselves and for all who, if we live, will be old along with us, and if we do not live may be old without us.

If we do not live . . . "Somewhere along the time-line," a friend wrote to us after the death of our daughter, "we begin to long for the love that lies ahead." And, in the words of another, "The resurrection takes on meaning for us when we begin to people heaven with our loves." Somewhere along the time-line, perhaps when one is middle-aged, perhaps sooner, perhaps later, depending on what our life experiences have given us and made us yearn for, if we are blessed with faith and hope and a speculative and adventurous mind and spirit, we begin to sense in a differently qualitative way that, while life is gorgeous, a gift of dazzling light and beauty as well as of terrible pain—and they are all bound together—and while most of us would not hurry our exit from life by one jot or one tittle, death is its own high adventure. We dare to hope in a new beginning, and that death, in that unknowable moment when it will come to us, will come as a friend.

5

Relationships—

After All This Time

For many of us in middle life, relationships may appear to take on new meanings, new colorations. It is not that they are more important, but perhaps they are more "chosen." The givenness of our biological ties begins to thin down, and we have both the time and the need to "cultivate" our friendships —that strange and apt metaphor of a gardener, stirring up soil around the roots of plants. Relationships with marriage partners, too, enter a new phase as the proportions of our common agenda shift away from preoccupation with children to other aspects of our common life. If we have moved, we have had to start all over again to find meaningful relationships in our new community. This may take a little more conscious effort than it once did when parents in the PTA, the neighbors on the street whose children played with ours, or the other parents in Sunday school were a ready-made pool in which to put out our feelers and find our congenial counterparts.

There are relationships that are not chosen, that are part of the psychic cells of our nature, and they, too, have their special meaning at this time in our lives. I refer to our relationship to those persons, including ourselves, who inhabited our childhood. By middle life we see these figures in a new way as we look back over time and perceive ourselves unequivocally as persons with a past.

Of course we always had a past, though it may be hard to remember that now. My son, at about eleven, got out his series of annual school pictures and lined them up. "I thought I'd see how I'm changing through the years," he said, and it startled me. Already? Does he know already that he has a past? Then I remembered how, at eleven, the past seemed very long, the future stretched ahead incomprehensibly. But now neither thing is true. The future is certainly not endless and the past is compressed, metamorphosed into crystalline jewels and flaws and continuums. Those people back there, frozen into those crystallized years—who were they, and who are they to me now?

Recently, helping my sisters and brother clear out the house where our parents had lived for nearly half a century, I came upon a log the nurses had kept of my long and critical childhood illness, that major event in my childhood that had such an effect in shaping the person I was to become. The medical chart—dots and lines in jagged succession—tells a grim story, of high fevers and rapid pulse and respirations, until on the 46th day I was taken to the hospital for emergency surgery in a last gambling attempt to save my life. The nurse's notes on the accompanying pages are even more harrowing: "Irrational all the time . . . very weak . . . irritable . . . respirations shallow and occasional deep sighing . . . Lips pale . . . Cried out sharply as if in pain." Then, moment of compressed terror and truth: "July 11. To hospital 7:30 P.M. To O.R. 8:15–ret.8:55 condition fair." After that the notations begin to take on the child again; "Comfortable . . . irritable all morning . . . very cheerful . . . on sunporch one hour. Playing comfortably most of the time . . . " How my spirit relaxes, relieved, even to read it all these years later. I come to the second last entry in the book: "Very cheerful all the time. Condition good." Then the last—a look to the future now that it seems assured I will have one—"Have Dr. Allen look at teeth."

Well, I have now read for the first time that book in its brown pasteboard cover. Why now? (It has been on that closet shelf since I was six years old.) Why have I read it at all? Was it to get in touch with that child, now that I am middle-aged and the home of my childhood is being broken up? My heart aches for my parents, back then, in their anguished watching and caring through those months, and for the child "weak, irritable, with occasional deep sighing." Who is she to me? I have other symbols of that childhood—toys, photographs, cherished books. I have a picture of myself standing in front of the spirea bushes. I am wearing the yellow chiffon dress my mother made for Easter, and I am smiling smugly. I wonder what it was about. Who was that, back there, when the nation was struggling with the Depression and there was no television and cars had square lines and were dark colors, and on the street where I lived there were daisies blooming in empty lots and the only sidewalk was made of large crumbly cinders?

The others who inhabited the house of my childhood with me—who are they? I see my mother, with her gifted hands, taking the afternoon to fashion for my sister and me two canopied doll beds made from cigar boxes, glue, empty spools, and strips of pink ruffled organdy and I see the three of us sitting around the dining room table where she is working and it is a feast of love and skill and fantasy. I see how the small white mattress fits exactly into the pink ruffled frame. I see my doll, bought at Watch Hill, Rhode Island, on a summer afternoon, lying on the pink and white bed, her shiny china face and painted black hair and china shoulders set onto a sewn cloth body. Into all that fantasy goes a book I had read of a doll, Hitty, that had lasted a hundred years. And into it also go images of queens and princesses who slept on piles of mattresses but knew that a pea lay under the whole pile, and the fantasy of myself, grown up, somehow beautiful and fair, lying on some bed as luxurious as this and knowing that the world is beautiful and fair and made for everyone else in the world, of course, but also made for me.

I see my father, wielding a shaving brush with an ivory and black handle, lathering his chin in the bathroom—the door is open into the hall—and singing! "Oh, sometimes I live in the city," my father sings, "And sometimes I live in the town." He takes a deep breath and, in exaggerated basso, sings on—"And sometimes the wild notion comes into my head"—another breath and a pause, for lathering, and for dramatic effect—"to jump in the river"—now, very deep tones—"and drown." I love to hear it. I hear it now, a symbol of my father, sharing his delight in the morning and in his life, with this hammed-up version of a song from his college days.

I see my sisters—the one so close to me in age that it is sometimes hard for me to see that we were two people, not one—best friend and most threatening competitor for love and attention. I remember her being willing, either out of my intimidation or her own sleepiness, to sit groggily against the edge of the bathtub and wait for me because I was afraid to get up and go to the bathroom by myself. I see my other sister, eleven years younger, almost *my* baby, obligingly letting me dress her in ruffly clothes and sit her in the Victorian chair I had carried out to the front lawn, so I could practice my new passion for taking photographs with the old box camera I had discovered in the cupboard.

I see my brother, born when I was nearly six and still recovering from my illness, so that I saw in him both a lovely companion, plaything, to help while away the hours I had to spend in bed and also an usurper of some of the love and attention my parents had showered upon me in my extremity and now, overjoyed at my recovering and at the advent of their first son, had diverted to him. I remember—a life guilt—an act of vengeance I inflicted on him when he was, perhaps, seven and I twelve. We went together to an annual fair and saw for the first time a small gyroscope. We were enchanted with it and discovered there were gyroscopes for sale. I had money with me but my brother had left his at home and I bought one but refused to lend him money—not because I needed it for other purchases at the Fair, only because—evil though I knew it to be—I did not want him to have one. The sins of childhood, will they ever leave us? "The remembrance of them is grievous unto us." My brother is now a physicist and I have speculated in a moment of whimsy whether that gyroscope was so compelling a toy for him when he was seven because he had a bent for physics even then or whether there exists in the complex of his motives for being a physicist a tiny aspect that says to me, See, I can have my gyroscope. And I can work it better than you can.

A few years ago, in an attempt to loose that particular demon, I sent my brother a small gyroscope for his birthday. It was half in jest and half in desperate earnest, but it did not work, not for me. I still cringe to think of myself, twelve years old, walking the dirt floors under the big roof at the Fair, unyielding to my brother's plea to lend him fifty cents.

There is a sense in which the gyroscopes from the past years continue to spin toward us, sometimes wobbly and wandering, but with us yet. There is also a way in which those years stand in a clearing alone. By the time we have reached middle life we are far enough from them to know they are separate from us and yet close enough to see, perhaps for the first time, how the child we were continues to form the adult we are still becoming. There is a favorite quotation of mine and it has become a favorite only in the last few years as I have had time and need to examine again part of the configuration of the person who, eventually, got up from that bed of convalescence and tried to catch up with the world outside, and to compensate for and continue to draw upon that crucible of lost and treasured time. The quotation is this: "Your childhood is like a bucket that you turn upside down over your head and it continues to pour down over you the rest of your life." I do not recall its source—only, now, that it is mine. At what age (nine? twelve? fourteen?) do we pick up the bucket, turn it upside down and begin to notice how it flows down over us? Perhaps we set it aside for awhile, during those compressed years of adolescence, or are at least mindless of its flowing, and it is only after some time has passed that we begin to notice how new occasions return us to old ones, new friends assume a part of the mantle of old friends, and how the smell of lilacs will take us back to the side hill behind our childhood home where we played "house" and "store" in the long afternoons, and set our sandcakes on the windowsill to cook in the sun.

We need to know about one another, the child each of us was, and to share our own pasts, too. When our young people get out the photo albums, show their friends their childhood photos, I know the friend who is looking is important. The old things we save—old toys, photos, a favorite dress—are for ourselves, of course, but they are also for the others who will become important in our lives. See, they say, this is what I was like before you knew me. During a period of many months when my daughter was small, a part of her bedtime ritual often included variations on the question, "When you were a little girl . . . what were your dresses like? What was your hairdo? What was your furniture like?" It was a favorite part of the ritual for me, too. We are grateful in a startled, hungry way when someone says to us, "What were you like when you were small?"

So we continue to draw from our childhood, to return to it as to a different world, as though the landscape of childhood, compelling, insistent, lies across some moat which, to cross over, is to enter a world where sums are never added but always multiplied and a grain of sand assumes the meaning of a universe and nothing is ever lost but lies there waiting, compounding its meaning in the unknowing brilliant shadow and light.

But not all our childhood associations exist back there in some world across the moat. There are continuities between ourselves and those people—there must be since, though our tissues change, we do inhabit the same body through all these years, and our small sisters and brothers grow to maturity, even as we. Yet there are times when it seems a charade—though the years and the mirror and all objective evidence tell us we are grownup, it startles us to find that this is so. My "baby sister" grew up to be, for awhile, a pension trust analyst, my older sister traveled with relief missions to Gaza—who could believe it? Visiting a university, I watch my brother—the college calendar says he is a visiting lecturer—deliver a lecture on low temperature physics and, tall and bearded, he stalks across the platform, visibly enjoying and struggling with the subject, and he writes figures and graphs on the blackboard and I do not understand the fine points of what he is saying but I do quicken to the trustworthiness and beauty of the microscopic world he is describing. But it seems he should be turning on the radio for Jack Armstrong the All American Boy or writing from a camp in Maine how he is taking Missionary Heroes and Stamp Collecting "because there isn't any Nature Study," or reading to us the Riddles and Posers from the Sunday paper.

Are we surprised to be grownups? Do we feel we have pulled off some coup to have become adults—parents, even —those persons who seemed to us in our childhood to wield such power? A few years ago we had a brief discussion in our family about whether to replace or refinish our second generation dining room furniture. The discussion ended with a decision to refinish after my husband said, "I grew up with this furniture and now *I'm* sitting in the father's chair!" My mother says to me, after I have expressed to her some surprise that I have been able to accomplish some ordinary but unmistakably grown-up task, "Martha, there are times, still, when I think, Now wouldn't my mother be proud of me!" How can we be grown-ups when our sense of ourselves as children sits there, intense and demanding, in the mind?

Our brothers and sisters do inhabit both our worlds, and help act out for us the continuity of our life. In our family we gather together when we can—husbands, wives, children—for a week of summer reunion, for recall, for catching up with each other, and because we like to be together. We gather in times of family crisis—"How do people manage who don't have brothers and sisters?" my sister says on the way to the airport as we disperse after the death of our father. And if tragedy befalls one of us and we call to impart our terrible news and a voice a thousand miles away on the other end of the line says without hesitation, "I will come," how the parenting arms of our common childhood are wrapped around us to say in some mysterious and ineffable way, "There, there, it's going to be all right."

But it is not only with the persons of early childhood that old relationships persist. I had occasion a few years ago to attend the 25th reunion of my high school class. I approached it with some trepidation. I had kept only the most tenuous connection with any of my high school friends, and for all these intervening years had lived away from the town in which I had grown up. The reunion turned out to be an occasion of unmitigated delight. How free we were able to be with one another! For one thing, there was no concern about age—who was older? who was younger? We knew we had all been seventeen twenty-five years ago and at most a year kept us all from being forty-two. Old anxieties—who is popular? who is bright? who is dating and who is not? who has pimples or braces or oily hair?—were all gone. For good or ill, we had come to terms with those questions. The boy who had sat across from me in French class and ran pins through the epidermis of his fingertips for my amusement and horror had become a policeman and added twenty pounds to his boyish frame. He said, as I approached him with some remnants of my old misgivings—Do they like me? Am I popular enough to get by?—"Martha, darling, how are you?" How good it felt, to enjoy these old friends, free of the anxieties of adolescence. How proud we were of the speaker of the evening—our classmate, an honor student back then and now editor of a newspaper. He was eloquent and insightful and when my parents sent me the local paper in which his speech had been reprinted, it read as well as it had sounded. But he could have done much less well and still have been a hero of the evening to us. When he said, reviving the parade of memories that had come to him in contemplation of this evening, "You were all beautiful. All wonderful," of course we believed him. Had we not endured as wayfarers and travelers out of that shared past for twenty-five years?

I met, on another trip home, a friend of long ago. We met inadvertently, in a hospital corridor. We had been in Sunday school together for many years, never in the daily close association of public school. Our parents had continued to be friends, but we had not seen each other in probably twenty years. We knew who each other were—a gracious acknowledgment that neither she nor I had become unrecognizable. Tragedies had come to each of us during those years and we knew that about one another, though we had never written. We spoke one another's names, and met in an embrace. And what we met, standing there wordlessly with our arms around each other, was some recognition of the flow of time and our common history in it, in this "home town" which she had stayed with and I had left, and in those ventures of life in which each of us had participated all unknowing of one another but going back into a nurture from which we will be fed for as long as we live. I do not know what this woman's interests are, or her accomplishments, or whether, were we to meet as strangers, we would be drawn to one another at all. It does not matter.

There are other "old friends" with whom we do continue to share common interests. I see after twenty years a man I used to know during my childhood and when we were students together. He has achieved eminence in his field of academic life and we would, if we had time, find much of common

interest to share. But there is, in our occasional chance meetings, an instant "catch-up" of our valuing of one another—as
though the capital of our relationship was established a long
time ago, and the interest has gone on compounding all
independently of whether we see one another or not. It is all
there, ready for the claiming, whenever we have a chance to
use it.

So much for the "old friends." What about the new? What
if we have moved and have to start over? Even if we have
stayed in the same place, there is more time available and we
do meet new people with whom we would like to become
friends. How do we manage, after by some process of tentative
mutual attraction we have found some prospective new
friends, to fill in the blank spaces in those friendships quickly,
to give them extra dimension and depth? Occasionally, by
some alchemy that seems to defy analysis we encounter someone with whom we discover a congeniality so startling and
immediate that we may wonder whether we were friends in
some previous incarnation. If we look carefully we may discover that such a friend reminds us of a loved sister or a childhood hero, or that this friend is so much like ourselves that in
some perhaps narcissistic way we may be loving ourselves in
that other person—or, to put it in a more kindly way, perhaps
because the person is so much like us, we can appreciate and
understand her so well.

But to develop a new relationship usually takes longer than
this instant recognition. Let me suggest three ways in which
new friendships may take on some of the qualities of friendships that have evolved over years. Often these three are all in
operation and that, I suppose, works best of all. The first is the
discovery of a common history and tradition. This can go all the
way from acquaintances who discover that both their families
used to summer in Maine to friends who learn that both their
grandfathers were rabbis and that they share a cultural and
religious identity that goes back to Abraham, Isaac, Ruth, and
Naomi. It is not just for common values and congeniality that
we often seek our new friends in churches and synagogues.
The sedimented rituals of our lives echo in these places and
the people we meet here participate, if only by their physical
presence, in the long echoes of these rituals. Or we may find

our common past in the repudiation of aspects of our heritage. A Unitarian friend tells me that much of the bonding in the congregation of which she is a member is built on a common repudiation of more orthodox religious history.

Often the items of common history are seemingly incidental and while having them in common hardly guarantees friendship it may make us easier with one another and able to get on with greater things. I refer to such commonalities as that bobby socks and saddle shoes were part of our peer uniform, or that we remember the speeches of Winston Churchill. That the popular songs of our youth are important bonds is obvious any time we go to a restaurant or a dance which caters to people our age and observe how the band plays "our songs" and how we smile at one another and are glad.

Other kinds of common history have nothing to do with institutions or group memories. Because I have had since childhood a sense of the fragility of life I feel an immediate kinship with anyone in precarious health, so that I have to be careful not to confuse or alarm such a new acquaintance who does not understand, after all, that we are seven degrees farther along in our friendship than she or he would normally expect. I have, now, a kinship with any parent who has lost a child through sudden violent death and, recently, after several days of struggle I wrote to the parents of a young woman such as this, about whose death I had read in the paper. In due time a note came back from the girl's mother. "We would love to know you," she wrote. "Dear friends are often born of tragedy." I know—had I not acquired an intimate friend in a woman I met last fall who told me that her son had been killed in a motorcycle accident the summer before?

A second way in which we may begin to telescope into a short time the development of a new friendship is through the discovery of common agenda, of common commitments. This is often a matter of history, but of present involvement, too, and it can be a commonality of profession, of political involvement, or a common love of modern poetry, or that we are both struggling with letting go as our children leave home, or that we are fellow members of A.A. or the Sierra Club. The attempt to find common interests can often be rather deadly, as anyone knows who has sat through discussions of cars, football, child exploits, or church politics and has no interest in these things. Nonetheless, we are hopefully trying to find each other in all of this, and if we are brave and imaginative we may strike paydirt in time to keep from falling asleep or wishing we had stayed home with a good book.

A third way in which we often speed up the development of friendships is in the kinds of intentional pressure-cooker experiences characterized by the human potential movement. This can go all the way from a structured sharing of significant data from one's past—"How did you heat your house when you were eleven years old?" "Who was the warmest person you knew when you were small?"—to a weekend or longer period of time in which a group of people through word and action and being quiet together try to disclose, comfort, explore, love, themselves and each other, with only a minimum amount of time away from one another for the necessities of physical self-maintenance. This is a volatile and relatively new way of growing in human relationships, and can be dangerous and also tremendously exciting and rewarding. At a time when people move around a great deal and we must find friends quickly or do without, and when it is for most of us easy to meet our basic needs and we have leisure and sophistication enough to crave an enrichment of our experience, the human potential movement can help us a great deal—in practicing risk, and trust, in learning what works in human relationships and how to appropriate that for ourselves.

I have said a lot about relationships at middle life and have so far not said anything about that relationship which is more important than any other, our relationship to our partner. I am a woman and I have been married to the same man for nearly twenty-five years. It is, admittedly, a specialized perspective, though not uncommon. It is only out of that perspective that I can speak, though perhaps some of what I say may pertain to other arrangements, too. My husband and I have been through a lot together. I recall the words of James Thurber to the effect that love is not moonlight and roses and the first flush of romance; love is being married to someone for twenty years and having six children together. For my husband and me, our life together has included graduate school, varieties of work for him and for me, moves around the country, the births and raising of four children, the death of one of them, and relationships with our extended families and with other communities dear to us. It has included times of stress, dissatisfaction, anger, and pain with each other and ourselves, as well as with the events of our lives. It has included occasions of delight, transport, and adventures rich beyond our understanding and a continuity of shared experience so dense with associations that now there are times when no word need be spoken because the thought is already known. Marriage, someone has said, can bring us both our best and our worst times, and I suppose if it is not the best thing in our lives then perhaps it *is* the worst.

What is special about our relationship with our spouse at middle life? The most obvious fact is that we have a whole lot more time and emotional energy for each other, now that the children are grown and probably living somewhere else. For those whose children have been the main thing that has held them together, the leaving of the children may be a time of great emptiness and difficulty and they may find the marriage will no longer hold. For others it may mean a whole new carefreeness and joy in each other. With a feeling of accomplishment and pleasure in their children, with a security about their vocations which has hopefully come to them by now, with the freedom that comes with the lessening of household demands and with the richness of a long and varied relationship, they can be lovers and friends in a more attentive and undistracted and sustained way than they have ever been able to be before. What looked in prospect like a lonely time may prove instead to be a new beginning.

But it may take some doing. Even for couples whose relationship with one another has been good, the departure of the children will require big adjustments: their going creates a vacuum something else must fill, and it is certainly wise to anticipate this time and to have begun making the adjustments before it comes. Will it be a new job for the wife, new interests, more time to return to some of the things they enjoyed before they had children at all? Any time we face major shifts in our lives is a good and often a necessary time for taking stock of ourselves, including our marriage—the ways we communicate with each other, whether the goals we have for ourselves are compatible with the way we live our lives, day by day. I do not mean long-term goals, like what will we do when we retire, or will the car last for another two years or should we get a new one now? These things we do need to talk about, but I am talking about the "incidentals" of which our lives are made—taking some time each day to say to one another in some unmistakable way, How is it with you today? Will you tell me about yourself? I am listening. There are things about me that I need to tell you.

What I am talking about is a level of intimacy that sometimes gets short-changed in the busy years of raising a family. Now is the time to renew it. If couples are bored with each other, if they find their interaction, including their sex lives, no longer very exciting, it may be, of course, some basic incompatibility or failure to grow through the years in congenial ways, but it may also be a failure to communicate with one another on a deeply intentional level. This kind of intimacy does not "just happen." It should not be confused with physical intimacy, though of course all aspects of our lives together reflect upon each other and contribute their share to either the zest or the fatigue of the relationship. It may not even be everyone's need or style, but it is worth asking, at middle life: Does our relationship somehow need refreshing? And if it does, what can we do about it? This may be a time to enroll together in a community adult education course—often a mental health center will offer courses on enhancing relationships—or to read together one of the many available books on enriching marriage.

New research on sexual activity in the years from middle life on is reassuring, too. There does seem to be a lessening of the frequency of sex as persons advance into their later years, but no lessening of the intensity or joy of the sex experience. I suspect that the earlier suggestion that sex after middle life became more of a generalized comfortable warmth with each other was not an assessment of physiological or emotional need or possibility, but was more a concession to society's judgment about the appropriateness of experiencing pleasure with one's body now that the "real" function of sex, procreation, was no longer an issue. None of us can know, of course, what our timetables of aging will be. In the meantime—a phrase out of the past, known perhaps only to the not-so-young—full steam ahead!

There are other good things about life with one's partner in middle life. If the marriage has held together this long, and is good, there is a comfortable security in knowing that it probably will continue to hold together, though of course this is not always so. It should not lead us to complacency, that our marriage has survived and seems in good condition. But the fact that we have weathered a lot together—have been very angry and returned, have felt hurt and misunderstood, and returned, have gone through periods of feeling disenchanted with one another, and returned—does give us some confidence, some security, about our future together. Perhaps this need for security is peculiar to those middle-aged or older. Perhaps the young do not need security. Recently my husband and I along with a young couple in our family took a quiz, each of us independently, about what one wants from a sex relationship. It was of interest to us all that my husband and I had both checked "security" as one of our needs, and that neither of the young people had done so. I certainly do not want security at any cost, but if I can have it, along with variety, excitement, mutual enrichment, and a lot of other good things, I want it. It feels good to me.

One of the things that this rather long-time security about our partner, our marriage, our self, can mean to us is the freedom to enjoy close friendships with others—men, if we are women—women, if we are men—who may or may not be as close a friend to our partner as they are to us. This may be a matter of changing cultural climate, as well as greater security and self-knowledge born of long experience about ourselves as sexual persons, as wives and husbands. It may be a matter of time and energy to give to other people. Much has been written about this, and its dangers are obvious—witness the couple who advocate "open marriage" as a way of maintaining what they present as their own admirable marriage, and soon thereafter are divorced. It will really not do to say, as perhaps we tried to do in a former time, that our friendships with men and women other than our spouses were somehow not sexual in nature. Of course they are—our sexuality is part of our meaning to every man, woman, and child whom we meet and certainly a large part of our meaning to ourselves. It is one of life's very best gifts to us, and one of the ways we are able to reach out and enjoy each other, men and women alike.

There may be for us, wending our way through this land of enrichment and hazard, some uneasy moments. It is not always easy to sort out which are unnecessary taboos of a sexually ambivalent society and what are valid personal inhibitions. As one friend put it, one has to be more "inner directed." To be an adult is to make responsible choices. By the time one has reached middle life, if adulthood has not set in now, when will it?

Relationships—do they get easier? Do they get better? What do they mean to us? What if we lived in a world somehow psychically alone? It is a condition of extreme mental illness, but what if it were so for all of us? What if the tangle of relationships in which we live were not present at all, but we somehow existed side by side, a mass of most uncompanionable beings? It is, to me, one of the miracles of life, given our physiological anatomy—we are, each, after all, enclosed in our own skin, supported by our own skeleton, given that ego drive within us that would, as infants, bring all the world to our doorstep to meet our needs—that we are able to understand and reach out to one another at all. It is one of the greater miracles of grace.

That there are times when we try to understand and love each other and fail terribly, we know. And that there are other times when we do not even try—we know that, too. Yet we hope. Some rising in us persists, longing for a community where all is known and loved, and when that happens the holy moment sheds its light back through history and forward into the unknown and all we know is this moment and it is enough.

Does it tell us something about our destiny, this longing for worlds of which we have tantalizing and graceful glimpses? The anthropologist Ashley Montagu speaks of coming out of the theatre after witnessing a play and of how the audience is united in a kind of psychic bond, a unity, which, he suggests, may be a foretaste of development to come. The Roman Catholic theologian, Teilhard de Chardin, speaks of a unity of consciousness, a higher level of community, toward which we

may be moving, in a developmental way. They seem far-off—
these prospects of perfect community. Yet we have our moments here, metaphors, perhaps, of times to come. Sometimes,
gathered in the shadow of some great tragedy or some unut-
terable joy or in the presence of some simple unexpected
revelation, we know we have happened upon a new world in
the midst of this world. "The kingdom of God is in the midst
of you," Jesus said, and its nature is love. The voice of love is
our relationship to each other—men and women, husbands
and wives, children, lovers, groups of people, sometimes, even,
as Saint Francis knew, to tree and fire and sunlight.

"The kingdom of God is in the midst of you." A man rises to
his feet in a memorial service for a young woman. We have
talked about the woman, talked some about our Christian hope
in the face of tragedy, but there is something else here that he
wants to articulate. "I just want to bear witness," he says, "to
the love that is in this room," and in their hearts the people
nod because it is so—they could reach out and touch it with
their hands.

We remember these times, sometimes peg our lives to them,
and from time to time find them again, in our relationships
with one another. A passage from T. S. Eliot comes to mind:
"What life have you," Eliot writes, "if you have not life together? There is no life that is not lived in community. And no
community not lived in praise of God."

6

Touched Any Barks
of Trees Lately?

I have gone back to work. It is something many of us have done, are doing, though increasingly, through a strength I admire but can scarcely imagine—many women are successfully combining outside careers with that of raising children. But I stayed home while our four children were small and for a lot longer than that. I stayed home, working at home as our children got started in school, until they had all left their daily residence with us.

Now, against my expectations, I have gone back to work. But only part-time—I work in the afternoon, or rather, I go to my job in the afternoon. In the morning I write, which is my work.

One of the things my going back to work, even part-time, has meant for me is, of course, that I am under more time pressure than I have been, and I need to sort out what things to omit and what to insist upon—to myself first, for that is where the decision is really made. There are things I can give up. I can do the wash more efficiently. I can bake fewer "goodies"—my husband and I, vigilant against the middle-age droops, do not need them. I can give up watching much of the morning news show. I can give up an occasional afternoon nap. And I can certainly give up browsing around the shopping center.

The Growing Season

But I cannot give up the trees. So this morning, after waking while it is still dark and wondering how I was going to keep in touch with a part of myself I value very much and which the more loosely organized structure of my days before I started my job had allowed me to cultivate—that savoring and reflecting upon experience until one has drawn from it nearly all of its meaning—I took off a few minutes to go out and commune with "my" trees.

My trees stand in the backyard, a group of them along the line between our lot and the neighbors who disappear behind foliage every spring and emerge again in late fall. One of the trees stands close to the corner, by itself, a sentinel. At another place, there are two standing close together, Siamese trees, almost, joined at the base and, surely, in the intertwining of their underground roots. Until the agricultural extension man came to advise us about some sickly bushes in front of the house, I didn't know what kind of trees any of them were. After he had suggested that the position of the bushes shielded them too much from the rain and what they needed was more water, we walked around the rest of the yard. When we got to the backyard I said, "These trees"—not telling him they were shade and sway and meaning and drama and sources of squirrel and bird watching—"seem to be pretty healthy."

"That's because they're native to the region," he said. "Some of them are hackberry trees. I'm not sure what that one is over there, with the big leaf."

That was yesterday, and today the trees call to me and I go out. I do not need to know their names, though I am glad to know they are native to the region. I walk first toward the lone tree standing close to the corner. Looking up, I watch its bare branches stitching and swaying against the sky. As I get close, it is the tree's trunk that I see, and standing in its presence I lay the palm of my hand against it, fitting my fingers between the ridges in the gray green bark, pressing my fingertips into the grooves. The projecting ridges, long knobs of gray and green, follow the line of the tree. The top of each is a protruding mini-peak. They remind me, in microcosm, of the ridges of the South Dakota Badlands, layers of one ridge having their counterpart in the layers of another ridge across the valley floor—only here the valley floor is a half inch span of tree trunk. I move my hands farther up the tree's trunk and then I lean my shoulders and head against it and I feel the bark against my face. In my fantasy I see the cells pressing against one another inside this tree. The growth-in-containment that this tree trunk represents, drawing life up from the earth and in from the air and sun and giving it all back to us again but keeping its own self so visibly intact, so peculiarly itself—it is a model I crave for myself as my feet press against the earth and I consider that inside my house are the call of a multitude of gifts and duties and that this afternoon when I again "go back to work" I will lose for awhile all conscious sense of what this tree and I are to each other.

I go to my other trees, and I lay my hands on them, too, and I wait for a sense of them to come to me, and it does—who could have imagined the bark of a tree! Then I go to my bush in back of the clothesline—my own particular burning bush where one day soon after my daughter's death I came out in desolation to take in the sheets I had hung earlier in the morning in the blazing sunshine, and needing a sign but not expecting it then I received a revelation, an intimation of presence in a particular motion of leaves and air and a sense of being *visited*, of being upheld by that mysterious presence so that now when the desolation returns it is often to that day and those moments my mind returns, often only as a memory, for the joy, the inexpressible gladness did not last but the memory of it did. My bush—what was it that made the ends of your branches tremble for those many moments on a still afternoon? Was it my daughter, returned to reassure and comfort me? Was it God? Was it a random wind? Was it some whirling field of energy in which they dwelt and to which we all have continuities as yet undreamed of? Who can know?

The branches of the bush were green then, only green. Now there are red berries among them, or upon a few vagrant branches that hang down among this green. When I sit at my desk inside I can look through an inner doorway and through a room, and out through an outside window, onto just that spot of green leaves and red berries. My burning bush. I stand by it now and wonder—will my visitation come again, a sign renewed? But no, the bush is quiet, or wavers slightly to the same breeze that is fitfully moving about the rest of the yard.

The Growing Season

But up above I hear the sound of squirrels moving and I look up and there are two of them, chasing one another along a limb coming out from the center of a high tree. They leap along the branch, in some kind of joyous joint mission—or so it seems to me, my neck craned to watch them. The leader squirrel jumps along a branch that thins out, is about to end, and there is nothing beyond until, across a gap of three feet, the thinned-down branch of the next tree over begins its gentle arc inward to its own trunk. The first squirrel hesitates only a second, the branch drooping under her weight. Then she lets fly against the blue sky and she lands, and her new perch dips and returns and she clings to it and then begins to scamper inward along its length and I know she is safe. I have watched this drama—this leap of faith across blue sky—twenty times since we moved to this house two years ago and I still cannot see it without tears of joy—the squirrel made it! She took the risk, and she made it! Does it move me to elation each time because I am a more cautious animal and I would like to emulate my friends the squirrels more often than I am able? If I believed, could I walk on water? The squirrel could. I know she could.

The other squirrel—is it a mate? a friend? a playmate of the hour? He hesitates, and I wonder if he will turn back, miss out on the rest of the trip? But no, there he goes, a small thing hurtling against the sky. He lands and his body rolls to the underside of the limb, his feet clutch above him at the jumping branch—he rights himself, and proceeds along the limb. Bravo! little squirrel, and thank you, thank you a hundred times. My bushes. My trees—mine only in that I have infused them into myself, watching them, touching them, feeling them against my hand.

There are other trees. There is a large, towering tree partway up a knoll on an island at the confluence of the Mohawk and Hudson Rivers in eastern New York state. On that island years ago were: a Cluett Peabody shirt factory, and a farm, and beyond the farm a farm gate, and, reachable only through that gate, a long sprawl of pasture land and grass-covered hills and a grove of trees and, on one of the grassy level places, a small rather primitive house known during my childhood as "the camp." It was the summer house my grandfather had built for himself, his wife and daughter, during my mother's late adolescence and thereafter they spent their summers there.

My grandfather was an engineer at the factory, known as the Bleachery, on the other side of the island, down below the farm. My mother was married from that house, leaving its rustic gate to go to the Second Baptist Church of Troy to marry Mr. George Whitmore, a young lawyer from Massachusetts. After her marriage, my mother would return to visit her parents there, and to take my sister and me, to stay for perhaps a week at a time, after which my father would drive over the Berkshire hills, to take us back home. After her mother's death, my mother continued to go and sometimes the visits, including four children now, would extend to two weeks, to lighten my grandfather's loneliness. He continued to work at the Bleachery. He would go to work down the hill in the morning, return at noon with a small white enameled pail of steaming soup from the factory kitchen, and slices of square-cut bread. After lunch he would go back to work, to return again for supper around the oilcloth-covered round table under the overhanging kerosene lamp where we would eat and sit and talk and my mother would sew and we children would read or play table games as the darkness closed in around us and left us, illumined and close, under the lamp.

Across the roadway from the house was a steeply rising knoll of hillside and, halfway up it, was the great tree of which I spoke. Its roots veined down into the ground, making delineated small spaces in which children could sit and look out over the valley, their backs resting against the tree. My sister and I used to take our dolls over there and play "house"—that age-old role practice of children, imitating grownups and trying on for size and feel what they might one day become. When, years later as a young mother, I held my children in my arms, the feelings of motherhood and domesticity came as naturally to me as rain falling on the ground. I had experienced them long ago—among other places, in the shade of that tree, with my sister, on that island hillside.

We have not been back there, any of us, since my grandfather died. I learned from a clipping sent me from the *New York Times* that the island has been bought by the New York State Office of Parks and Recreation, as a "unique recreational, scenic, and historic resource." It was evidently much used by the Mohican Indians and later on as a site of fortifications during the Revolutionary War. It pleases me to have "our" island so illustrious, and if I let my imagination pick its own way, I can see Indians moving among the trees (probably the meadows were not cleared by then) and I can see young men, dressed like Washington Crossing the Delaware, building their fortifications. Where? Where the Bleachery stood? or the farm? or the gate? or "the camp"? My own list of historic sites would be somewhat different—the grayed house, the boat in the front yard filled with a spilling profusion of petunias, the washstand out in back where we would go to slap cold water on our faces in the morning—and my tree, that great towering tree with its angling-out roots where my sister and I played on summer afternoons.

There are trees in Massachusetts, too, that my fingers recall as I touch the barks of these trees here in my newly-adopted land of Tennessee. There is the third tree in a line of trees that my parents planted soon after they built the house in which I grew up. Now, forty years later, the trees have grown to different heights—as did the children, who grew up inside the house. The third tree overgrew the tallest. From its lowest limb, now high off the ground, my father hung a swing for his grandchildren. It is the tree we passed closest to on our thousands of walks from the front door to the car and back again. It is a special kin. I do not go back to my mother's house now (my father's house, too, though he has been dead for two years) that I do not, on the occasion of my walk around the yard, go to that tree and lay my hands upon it. It feeds me and, against all reason, I believe I nourish it, too.

There is another tree in that yard, at one end of a garden. It is a tall pine—grown so tall now that the first several yards of its trunk are bare of branches—the sun does not reach there and the growth has moved upward. My father brought that tree from a New Hampshire mountainside where, along the shores of a small, crystalline lake, our family vacationed for many years when I was young. I have loved that place, and to have a tree from there, brought small and grown large, in my father's garden pleases me beyond words to tell about it.

There is something else about that tree, transplanted from

New Hampshire, and it may be one key as to why trees are my friends and loves. I did not discover this key until recently when, plagued by the uneasinesses of some of the changes of middle life I entered into a series of counseling sessions and, in the process of some old recall, came upon that part of my story. One summer, after my long childhood illness, when I was, though guardedly, well again, I went with my family to that New Hampshire mountain and lakeshore. I was not allowed to go swimming yet, as a precaution against recurring heart weakness, so I had to find other pleasures. And I did, with the help of my friend Shirley who, although several years my senior, took it upon herself to befriend me. We spent a lot of time—Shirley and I—playing with dolls and pine cones and pine needle chains among the woods that stretched along that lakeshore, cleared only for the cabins in which we slept and ate, and for a rough roadway, and a central grassy area where, every afternoon after a midday dinner, the men of the vacation compound would gather and pitch horseshoes, and the women and children would sit on the wide wooden steps of the main house, and the women would talk and the children munch candybars while the thwunk, thwunk, clang, thwunk of the horseshoes sounded out against the jocularities of the men and the rising of puffs of sand in the clear mountain air. But mainly the place was known by its trees and those trees—the smell and sight and feel of pine trees—became some kind of symbol of my delight that I was, in fact, alive, and out in the sun and trees again, and back to a place I had loved and, along with everything else I knew, almost lost. My trees. My return to life. My nourishment. My affirmation. I *believe* in trees, and when I read, of primitive religions, that their adherents believed there were gods residing in trees I think, Of course, why not? Have I not met them there?

But I am not through with them yet, my trees. They have a different meaning, too, and it is reflected in a poem by Robert Frost, "The Sound of the Trees," in which the poet describes the fixity of trees, their constant small noises reminding us of their presence, suggesting they are about to do something, but they never do—and then contrasting that with his personal resolve to make fewer noises and motions of resolve and preparation, and to be off ". . . I shall have less to say, But I shall be gone." I have gone back to the poem many times as, faced with some decision that was difficult to make, and looking for that extra nudge to move from contemplating the decision to making it, I have reread the poem: "They are that that talks of going but never gets away." I could be like that, talking of doing something—starting a book, learning to play the cello, undertaking a more faithful exercise program, even calling a friend to come to dinner—and never getting to it. The trees—buzz buzz, scrape, blow, whisper—remind me of that. It is their function to stand still; it is not mine. I like to have them remind me. I like it that I have "acquired a listening air" —newly acquired it, maybe, now that I have reached middle life—not only for trees, but for the whole range of natural sensory phenomena of which my hand on their bark is but one example.

There are others. I have begun to swim again. I always swim on summer vacations, since that waterless summer of my sixth year. But I swim other times now, in the local YMCA pool, with its fiberglass roof and glass walls that can be retracted when the sun shines bright and the air is warm. I swim for health, but also for the feel of water around me. I swim and when I am tired I lie back on the water and it supports me. It is a paradigm of trust and it rests my spirit as well as my body. In winter the water in the pool where I swim is heated and I recall with a forthright pleasure how as a child I had a fantasy of a bathtub big enough to swim in and now, lowering myself down the ladder into the huge warm expanse, my fantasy has come alive, and I take off in it, the water slowly churning in my wake.

Why, now that I am over forty, does the motion of my body through water please me so? Does the fact that I was never notably skillful in athletic events add a particular triumph to my skill now—see, I knew I was not clumsy and inept—this many years later? Am I freer to enjoy my body now than when the shadow of sickness still hung over me? ("Be careful—don't climb too many stairs." "Her heart has been weakened once, it could be again.") For us all, sick or well, was the task of becoming adults, of acclimating to all the bodily changes of adolescence and the new persons we had become, so demanding that we had to leave behind for awhile those childlike joys of reveling in sunshine and water, and put our full intent upon "growing up"? And those years between then and now—if, as I did, we married and had children—what happened then? when the children were small and growing up? Perhaps for those of us who have invested ourselves heavily in parenthood it is easy to lose sight of a part of ourselves, because our children absorb like water into blotting paper so much of our energy and awareness. Our delight is in *their* perception of rainbow oil on sidewalk puddles, in how *they* notice—and tell us about it—that if you lie on your back and hang your head down over the edge of a bed you think the world is upside down. Of course we remember how it was, but maybe it is our children's experience that trips our memory off. And that's fine, for awhile.

I have a series of snapshots I took of my daughter the second summer of her life. She was out in the backyard, and we lived in the country then, with pasture land surrounding our yard at the back and there she was—exulting in being alive! I turn to the pictures to be sure my memory is correct. It is—she is standing erect, her head slightly raised, her arms held away from her body—hearing it all, seeing it all, a world calling out to be noticed. There is another picture in the series where her arms are flung out, her body, in her small smocked dress, half turned—it is a dance of childhood, a dance of absorption and delight. I remember the occasion and my delight in it, and also that I was almost seeing it through my daughter's eyes, and feeling it in her muscles.

But now, my children grown, I am, in a sense, my own again. I go down to get the paper in the early morning. The freshness of a Tennessee morning in fall, or in spring, is an immersion—the sun, the birds, the trees, the bath of air. It is now I who hold my arms out to the morning, exulting in the feel of it. A car approaches down the road and I return my arms to my sides, but slowly—were *I* coming down the road I would be glad to see a middle-aged woman exulting in the morning.

The feel of things. A blind professor for whom I read one summer told me how he liked to work in his garden, and that he especially liked to raise eggplant, and he spoke of the feel of it in your hands. I remember visiting St. Louis and being taken to see the great steel arch that rises more than six hundred feet into the air above the riverbank and how, standing at the base of the arch and struck by its concept and by the sharp contrast of shadow and light where the plane of the arch column angled away from the sun, I put out my hand, to touch it. Perhaps, among art works, it is sculpture which most cries out for the sensing of our hands. Visiting some friends in a distant town, I am shown their recent acquisitions of several pieces of sculpture—two Eskimo soapstone carvings, a wooden sculpture of raccoons, and a fragile, long-legged bird. Because I am at home here I feel free to truly explore these sculptures with my hands, feeling stone and wood and metal, the planes and curves and angles beneath my hands. It takes me several minutes but I do not need to explain myself here, and when I am done, the husband of the family takes my hands in his and says, "I'm glad you've come," and part of what he is telling me is what I know—that I am loved and welcomed in this house, and part of it is an acknowledgment of our mutual gratitude for the feel and texture of life, perceived through the human hand, and for, in fact, the whole sensory world, which moves us, instructs us, and brings us its elation and its pain.

For some it is sounds that bring the revelation. Andre Kostelanetz, quoted in the *New York Journal American*, says: "The wind is one of my sounds. A lonely sound, perhaps, but soothing. Everybody should have his personal sounds to listen for—sounds that will make him exhilarated and alive, or quiet and calm. As a matter of fact, one of the greatest sounds—and to me it is a sound—is utter, complete silence."

Some use pictures. The photographer, Edward Steichen, tells in his book, *A Life in Photography*: "One spring, from the window of my bedroom I noticed a little shad-blow tree in full bloom. I remembered I had planted the tree twenty or twenty-five years before, when it was no more than a foot high, but this was the first time I had observed it in bloom. From then on, I concentrated on the little shad-blow tree. For the next three or four years, I photographed it on 35-mm color film in every season and at all hours of the day." He continues on to say that when he had finished he had "several hundred pictures of the little shad-blow." Several hundred pictures of one tree! One thinks of paintings—of Van Gogh and his sundrenched canvasses, or of Rembrandt and his illuminations of light and shadow.

Some use words. The poet and novelist, James Dickey, tells how, in preparing to write about the ambiances and character of the South, a land he knew and loved, he would not deal with anything he had merely *seen*. "Only what I *behold*, will I put in my book." Annie Dillard writes in *Pilgrim at Tinker Creek:* "Seeing is of course very much a matter of verbalization. Unless I call my attention to what passes before my eyes, I simply won't see it. It is, as Ruskin says, 'not merely unnoticed, but in the full, clear sense of the word, unseen.' . . . I have to say the words, describe what I'm seeing."

For some, revelation comes in other forms. The author G.K. Chesterton, in his book on Saint Francis, describes Francis as walking around in a state of perpetual wonderment, as though the world were upside down and it was some kind of continuing miracle that the mountains did not, therefore, fall into the sea, or the trees fall down from the sky. Behold! Look around! See! I recall my small son saying to his father, "Why doesn't everybody thank God for the world? They know they're on it, don't they?"

What gives us the power to unveil our lives—to perceive the world as though for the first time? For children, it *is* the first time. For Saint Francis, it was the indwelling of Christ that made a state of wonder apparently a kind of norm in his life. For some, a life-threatening illness will strip the scales from their eyes. For Annie Dillard, James Dickey, and Edward Steichen, it is the artist's special vision. For us at middle life, it may be several of these things, compounded, perhaps, by a new freedom of time and emotional energy, that sets us free to wander over the sensations of the world and to find them, again, good. There is something else, and that is the knowledge we carry in our bones that we do not have forever in which to soak up—through the nerve endings of these cells, the rods and cones of these eyes, the tympani of these ears—the wonders of the earth, and the sadness and urgency of that may give us new appreciation for the feel of life upon our hands.

Two summers ago we went to Colorado for our two weeks of vacation-family reunion. The place where we stayed was a mountainside compound of lodge, cottages, stable, meadows and trees, facing toward the snow-pocked cliffs of Long's Peak, and the expanses of Rocky Mountain National Park where the windings of Trail Ridge Road move a steady stream of visitors among the trees and cliffs and tundra of this high land. I had been to the Rockies before, two years earlier, for a briefer time. I remembered the ride along the ridges and how the children had got out and climbed to so many cliff-edges and how I, my heart in my throat, had turned away each time so I would not see them standing at the tops of a dozen drops of thousands of feet until by the end of the day I had cried hysterically at scarcely more than an imagined slight because my nerves were so frayed by the height and the cliffs and the spectre of disaster, of falling and death.

Now, two years later, we had all returned, and I thought I understood a little more the causes of my fears and that I would manage better this year and I, too, after all, was moved by the majesty and grandeur of these mountains. But on our first morning there, it was to the meadows outside the lodge that I went—my own search for a kind of intimacy with these mountains that I could begin on in my own way.

The flowers here are new to me—the land is high and the climate different from any place I have lived and if I saw these flowers two years ago I do not remember them. I pick my way carefully through the tall grass and stones—the ground is uneven and I do not want to step into an unseen hole. Into the meadow, and surrounded by flowers, I stoop to be close to them, to run my fingertips over a mustard yellow center, pebbly and coarse, to slip my fingers up the shafts of a long green spray speckled with crimson the color of drops of blood along its stem. There is a silky green flower here, like a fox glove and it, too, absorbs all the light my eyes can focus upon it. There is a white lacy plant, like Queen Anne's lace, but of smaller diameter. I lay my palm gently on the lacy dome, move it off. There are shafts of small purple bells. I do not know their names. They do not know mine. It does not matter. For a moment I look away from my flowers, though my hand is still upon them, up toward the high mountains, the high, craggy magnificent shapes, up, up, miles above my head. But it is not for them that tears of gratitude spring to my eyes. It is not for them that my heart lifts and sings. It is for the flowers I stoop among and lay my fingers upon. It is for this meadow, and the skin of my hand to touch it, and the sight of my eyes to see it. The words of A. E. Housman come to mind: ". . . Now of my three score years and ten Twenty will not come again . . . And since to look at things in bloom, Fifty springs is little room, About the woodlands I will go To see the cherry hung with snow." At twenty, and doing a narrative poem as my college senior honor project, I had used that poem as an introduction to my work, and the words became mine. I appropriated them, and they have returned to me often and now, more than twice twenty, I hear them again.

After a few days the mountains have become my friends. I sit on the porch and, looking out over the meadows and the small bright flowers, I feel at ease with the mountains, too, though I shall not scale them, or be able to lay my hands upon them.

The days pass and within a week my daughter is dead and the feel of her hands on these mountain flowers or on the stone geode-butterfly she had, on the day before she died, bought for her great-grandmother—the feel of her hands on these wonders, or the feel of her arms around my shoulders—the rich perceptions of her body, will be no more. And I think of the poem of Housman again and of my communion with the wildflowers on that mountain meadow and of how I, in middle life, have felt so sharply the beauty of the world, against a knowledge that our bodies, our senses, are all doomed by time. Yes, I believe in other worlds to come, but this world is what we have loved. I recall the words of Camus, cataloguing the delights of the senses and then saying, "What is eternity to me?" and I feel the loss, a terrible pain.

There are hopeful things that have come to us, too, in these flowers, in the tenacity of the tundra higher up, clinging to the high rock, the fragile beauty of mountain flowers, here for a season—or a day—and then gone.

When we went to leave this place we took with us, pressed between the pages of a book, a few flowers—white, golden, purple, green—gathered from the meadow outside of our cabin. I do not know all that they symbolized for us—only that we needed them.

Months later, finding the world beautiful again though full

101

of pain, I went outside to commune with my trees. I stood for awhile with my hands on each of two trees and I felt the energy of life flowing through us all. I felt with my hands again how the jagged ridges of bark lay in their marvelous patterns up and down the tree's trunk and looking at them I remembered the first time I flew in an airplane over the Allegheny Mountains and how, looking down from very high up, the mountain ridges looked like the grooves on this tree beneath my hand in this corner of my backyard in Tennessee, and I noticed how the green lichen, its edges paling and scalloped, was both blemish and design on my tree. Looking down I saw where a tendril branch had sprung from the base trunk and curled out into the air for awhile and then curled back toward the trunk at the level of my hand, and had evidently rested itself against the ridge of bark long enough for the teeth of the ridge to grow around it, lightly, and then the tendril had swung away again, gone off on its own, and was growing free, up into the air. It comforts me—my tree, this tendril, somehow a symbol of my daughter. I realize again, standing here, how the air hums with proclamation—my trees, this tendril, the yard, the bushes of my visitation. They are themselves—the tree-ness of trees, the bush-ness of bushes. They are also my symbols.

What are yours? Listen for them. Find them. Feel them beneath your hand. They will breathe with your breath. They will dance to the rhythm of your blood. They will sing out—a chorus or a hum. What will they say? Pay attention? Look? Listen? Feel? Yes, all of that. And something more. Life is a gift, they will say. Love is its meaning. Therefore love, they will say. Love us all. Love each other. Love yourself, you are worthy. Love the living. Love the dead. You will receive an hundredfold —sight for your eyes, balm for your pain, hope for your despair, the feel of trees beneath your fingers. You will receive— incredible promise—"beauty for ashes, the oil of joy for mourning, the garment of praise for the spirit of heaviness."

Have *you* touched any barks of trees lately?

7

Faith

and Personal History

"Theology," someone has said, "begins with a cry." Or, as Robert Frost said of poetry, with a lump in the throat. Or with some gladness one does not know what to do with, and casts about looking for a sound or a word or a concept into which to put the inexpressible.

We make varied attempts to express the inexpressible—we who are driven, or gifted, by some need to describe and therefore to begin to understand our lives. Some of us make systems out of it—write dogmatic treatises in which at least most things seem to fit or, if they do not fit, we claim the word "paradox" and systematize that. Perhaps our system may save us, be a stay against darkness and a form which organizes, even a little bit, the data of our lives and by giving us understanding, may make us seem less fragile, less lost.

We may try, through sensory awareness techniques, or through trying to abstract ourselves from our senses, to get in touch with some essence of life, and to celebrate that, and to show others the way to that, either in words or in silences. "Om—" the eastern chant vibrates into the air and it occurs to me wryly, only after I have joined in that chant a number of times and felt a kind of abstract purity in it, that the sound is so similar to our word, "home."

Or we may try another way, the path of myth-writers and

The Growing Season

Old Testament scribes, and writers of religious confessions and poets and novelists and of the nine-year-old child I had in a writing class who wrote out her fears in a story of flood and catastrophe—"When I was thirteen," the story began. It is the way of the storyteller.

We can tell our stories in archetypal terms, looking back over our knowledge of history and our knowledge of our own experiences and, as perhaps the Old Testament writers did, make our surmises. How could it be, any of it—the marvels of water, light, dark, animal, man, woman? Why do we suffer? How did it all get started? My son, very small, his imagination set to whirling, said to me one day, "I wonder, wonder, wonder, who made God?" Who can deal with such questions? "And the spirit of God moved upon the face of the waters"—it is as good a way as we know for expressing, conjecturing about, the inexpressible, and surely some special insight, some tying of causality to the symbols of everyday, must have come to the first person who wrote down the words. "And the evening and the morning were the first day . . . and God saw everything that he had made and behold, it was very good." Understatement of the eon, we might think, but how does one talk about it—creation, day and night, life? And yet we need to, sentient, knowledgeable, suffering, glad, and wondering as we are.

If we are neither theologians nor myth-writers, we are left with our own stories, transmuted into novel or play, or just written down as accounts of our lives—of what happened when we were young, and while we were growing up, and after we were grown—what happened then? It may be both the worst and the best way to write about faith—the worst because it seems presumptuous and we can get bogged down with a lot of trivia meaningful to us but not to anyone else and it all seems so personal. And the best for the very same reason—that it is as persons living in our everyday worlds that we are won or lost, despairing or hopeful, tied inside ourselves or enabled to care about others enough to risk ourselves for them. Yes, it is personal, and there is good precedent for that if we need it, our best message about the nature of God having come to us as a person who lived in a particular village, with particular family, and got dirty and tired and was awfully gratified when a woman "wasted" her precious oil because he needed so badly to have someone say, "Look, I care about you, I know you are special—let me take care of you for a change." The incarnation was God's message to us in our terms, very personal terms, which are what we most deeply understand.

How to write about faith, then, in the personal stuff of everyday—in the stuff of love and relationships and growing older and houses and moving and children and wondering about death, and of trusting way beyond what you can get a hold of at the moment—the evening and the morning of each day's life? There is a way in which, wanting to write about faith, about how our faith is given to us and acted out by us in these terms of everyday innuendo and decision, my answer to my own question—How?—is, I already did. Like the composer who played a piece of music and was asked, "What does it mean?" and sat down and played it again. There is a sense in which one's faith is a mirror image of one's life. I think of the story of Medusa and how it was death to look upon her directly: only in a mirror could she be safely viewed. I think the symbol may often apply to faith, too—that too direct an approach—labels, analyses—may miss or confuse the viewer's religious perception altogether. It is a different thing to talk about religion than to understand one's self as a religious person. Both are useful, but they are different.

Yet I do want to talk about religion, about faith, to write about it, though in the terms of everyday events. Perhaps it is like taking those events and looking at them again in a different light—as rocks in a cave appear differently under regular spotlights than when an ultraviolet light is shined upon them. The rocks are the same, but the illumination under which we view them shows up different things, turns a gray stone to crystals of shimmering blue-violet.

Kierkegaard speaks of "living in the religious spirit" and likens it to floating on a deep sea over 70,000 fathoms of water. "No matter how long the religious man lies out there, it does not mean that little by little he will reach land again. He can become quieter, attain a sense of security, love jests and the merry mind. But to the last moment, he lies over 70,000 fathoms of water." To those of us addicted to religion, for whom religious understandings and questionings are as integral to our lives as the air we breathe, it seems that everyone floats on that sea, and if we are different in any way it is only in our acknowledgment of that and our attempt to learn how to float, and to look around, and go with the tides, and swim to the buoys if there are any, and believe in the land and its promise even though we may not see it.

Faith is a way of seeing, then, as well as of understanding, the events of our lives. Faith and personal history. Faith at middle life. There is a lot to say and it is frightening, because it is so important and one may say it wrong, kill it with overtalk, or speak too baldly of what can scarcely be touched at all lest its delicacy be violated and it retract and die. Yet it is exciting, and there are places where it takes off and flies and sings and they, too, must be spoken of or the truth will not be honored.

Let me stake out my territory and hope that, with this advance warning, you will stay with me. There are things that have to do with what our status is, both as we find ourselves now and as we look back over the histories of our lives to this point. I cannot in good conscience attempt to write about faith and personal history, in a book on middle life, without paying at least modest attention to these understandings of reason and form. They are rationally arrived at, which is not to say they are any less or more "religious" than other understandings. I hope they will help you—and me—to understand our lives at this stage. They are in black and white. They come through the left hemisphere of the brain—using the theory that rational experiences are mediated through the left side of our brain and mystical, intuitive experiences come through the right hemisphere.

There is another body of material—stories, hunches about religion, that are intuitive, nonrational, transcendent if you will. They relate—many of them but not all—to the death of my daughter because that is so much of what my story is now. I wonder—What have they to do with you, or with middle life? Only this: that the realization of death is perhaps *the* agenda of middle life—not, for most people, though for more than a few, the death of a child—but other kinds of death: the death of parents, the death of a particular kind of relationship we have had with our children, perhaps the death of some limitless hopes with which we have sustained ourselves until they will no longer hold, the death of our youth and any illusion that death will come to other people but not to us. There is rebirth in these events, too—make no mistake about it—rebirth, reincarnation, whatever symbol seems to suit. But that does not happen until a certain dying has taken place and we have accepted that in its final difficult terms, have taken that, embraced it, into our lives.

So an experience like mine, of the death of a child, while it has elements of tragedy and terror that are uniquely hard, is, in another way, the common experience of middle life.

"You must never tell people what to do," writes W. H. Auden in an essay on "The Good Life," "only tell them particular stories of particular people." Perhaps our stories to one another, of hope, revelation, and mystery, can help us as we go on our way. They are my "right hemisphere" stories, in living color. It is they that make my heart pound, that give me comfort in the night watches and hope for a future I cannot know. They tell me that *something is going on.* They have their counterparts in the stories of others—the disciples somehow reviving at Emmaus, Paul trying to interpret his strange experience in ways people could understand, Arthur Koestler writing about quantum physics and telepathy—and all simple unknown people who find that somehow attached to the jumbled code in which their lives are written there may be some other graphic scrawls, written in lemon juice, and that if you hold it all up to the light the strange scrawls assume the form of letters, and words, and the Word, the *Logos,* assumes some shape, blurred, clearer, clear, and the mysterious garble of scratches and lines—fits together! They are the Aha! of my life, my "soft evidence" that something is going on, and if I am to write about faith and personal history I must tell about them, too, for they are my story.

But first, on to the black and white. By the time we have reached middle life, we can see how our religious perspectives have grown out of our past experiences. Maybe now we are able to use the associations out of our past which are helpful as religious metaphors and to set aside those that are not. We have known for a long time about this interaction of faith and experience, and may try to "overcorrect" for it. Harvey Cox, in *Seduction of the Spirit,* points out how the work of young theologians is often full of this personal acknowledgment, but that as they get older, more established, their work tends to become less personal, more abstract and "protected." Cox suggests that we would do well to stay closer to ourselves and our histories in our religious speculation, and to recognize how densely faith and experience are bound together.

If we watch, we see this interaction every day of our lives. A guest preacher gives a sermon full of authoritarian symbols of obeying and disobeying, of powerlessness to do anything but accept rules which make no sense to us. I cringe against such an understanding of God, but I remember that this man spends his vocational life working with prisoners in a system in which he sees capricious judgment and irrationality every day—of course he is affected by his surroundings. It is common knowledge that our use of "Father" as a term for God is heavily colored by our experience of our own fathers, and that if we have had a bad experience with our father we may have to find another term—like the man who referred to God as Sam. A woman I know whose father was a kind, loving, and just man but was away from home a lot when she was small tells me she thinks of God as kind, loving, and just but often not there when you need him. If I have been at times jealous of my brother, do I have a sense of sibling rivalry toward Jesus, too? "Jesus, our brother, kind and good," the song goes. Our symbols are loaded for us: they are imperfect vehicles for giving us a sense of perfect love, perfect justice, kindness, caring. Yet the symbols of relationships are the vehicles we have for understanding these things, and it all gets mixed up together.

For women, the symbols of faith may set up different currents and countercurrents than they do for men, and perhaps this comes to us with particular vividness as at middle life we move from becoming a nurturer of children and young persons to being somehow more located within ourselves. Women have got all embroiled in the servant-helper self-abdicating role which has been our traditional role, and which is also part of the message of Christianity: pour yourself out for others, be the servant, the person for others—which has often been, in turn, mixed up with relinquishing to someone else the major decisions of our lives. How do we find some content to the phrase "being obedient to the will of God" that does not do disservice to our need to stand on our own, to be free, to take such responsibility for ourselves as is appropriate to us? Who is to mediate the will of God to us? It is one of the important tenets of Protestantism that we all have access to God, in "the priesthood of all believers." Yet we are conditioned by our experience and in the absence of an authoritarian church, who will help us know the will of God? A father? A husband? The church? A male-dominated culture? Our own easily-aroused guilt feelings? We all know extreme stories of persons who try to manipulate others by putting a personal wish in terms of "God revealed to me—" that you should sell me your house for the expansion of this college, that you should come and live with me, even that it is "God's will" that our marriage be dissolved. We are rightly skeptical about revelation in these terms. But it takes awhile—maybe less long now that we have so much more consciousness about women's roles than we did twenty years ago—for us not to acquiesce in some of the subtler and therefore more dangerous manipulations of society. I heard of a woman minister who, after long discussion about the difficulties of women being whole persons in the church, was asked, "Why? Why do you stay with the church, in view of all that?" And she replied, quite simply, "I have this thing about Jesus." Granted we may look for, and find, in Jesus the attributes that support our particular skewness. (I who need to make myself known in human relationships think of Jesus as risk-taking. Another, who needs support for her righteous anger with society may think of Jesus as that figure driving the money-changers from the temple.) But we do not find, any of us, in the model of Jesus anything to subvert the humanity and dignity of any person—man or woman—under the sun. It is good to remember that, when we are struggling with issues of personal worth and who decides who shall be the servant and who the served. The decision to be servant, if it comes, must come out of abundance and freedom, not from intimidation or role-casting.

What about the shape our lives have taken as at mid-point we look back and see how events seem to have impinged on other events—"If you had not gone to that youth conference and you had not met Ray and you had not gone with him to that meeting and you had not met my sister, you and I would never have met each other." Do we see some causality in that?

The Growing Season

Do we see "the hand of God" in that? Do we see the same kinds of self-selection Darwin described in *The Origin of Species* and if that is what we see is not that, too, the hand of God? I must confess that I am not very comfortable with the notion that, in any small detailed way, God has a "plan for my life." The framework sounds too circumscribed, the drafting too specific, too linear. Maybe it is the issue of freedom again, and I resist the notion that a God who wills for me life and freedom would not prefer for me to "play it by ear" as events unfold. (If there is a plan, how am I to avoid thinking I could have done it better? And as for the "God knows best" retort, it smacks too much of the "Mother knows best" theme of childhood to be very convincing on a feeling level.) Perhaps if there is some kind of "plan" for me it exists in a network of dimensions and forces so vast and so unknowable that to label it "plan" belies its nature, short-changes life's mysteries and possibilities.

What does faith have to say to us as we come to terms with our careers, our life-achievements so far? I have dealt with this some on earlier pages, about a sense of freedom that may come when one stops putting a lot of energy into "climbing the ladder" and relaxes more into the appreciation of the now —when the process of life becomes its goal. I am a writer not because I hope to have written several books before I die— though that would be a gratifying by-product of my work— but because in the process of each day's work I discover myself, my life, my understanding of human experience, my resolution of pain, my comradeship with others, my belief that there is mystery and intention and we are all its observers and participants. If I write, my spirit quiets within me and if I do not, over a period of days and weeks, I am irritable, sad, feel a buildup of pressure which only a return to writing will dissipate. Walter Nash, in "Our Experience of Language," describes a writer's experience—and I hope that, for their adherents, many vocations have this quality of finding, and being found: "In language I make effigies and create ikons. In words, whispering, stumbling words, in the litter and ceaseless drift of words, is my searching for my own identity . . . till at last all burdens are laid down and I need no more words, not even amen and good-night." I write to understand, to "use myself up," and I think when I was functioning happily as a mother it was for the same reason—as well as for all the other reasons of love and procreation and duty and self-perpetuation and a belief that the world would be a better place because of these children.

The children would grow, for better or for worse. It was easy to see process as important then. The books will not assume maturity unless I am very diligent. The product—the end results—matter very much but it is still the process of the day (though it is sometimes tedious and I often drag myself to it) that gives me sustenance through the day. This realization has come to me more strongly in the last years as I have noticed with some surprise that the final arrival of a book or an article on the market is almost an afterthought—pleasant, delightful, gratifying—but that I am already into the next project and *that* is now "my work" and that if I have worked for a long time on something that I have not been able to sell, that work was still good work for me to do. It is the process and not the success of the final product that consumes me, burns through my life.

It is in a way a story that has repeated itself—my children, my books—and the second career has come to me as bonus, since I expected of myself only that I would achieve as a wife and mother and after that . . . an expectation of a kind of coasting, I guess. This pattern is changing for women and has always been different for men, who have begun their careers in the expectation that they would have to do a certain amount of "grub work" in their chosen fields and *then* they could begin to enjoy some achievement and success. So that maybe the "religious aspect" of work, of career, comes to them differently, and maybe it is harder, at middle life, for men, who may have to move from chasing receding goals to seeing process as the goal. But it seems very congruent with religious understanding to perceive the process, the Now, of our lives as what is holy, what is usable, what we need. "Behold, I make all things new." What that means to me, among other things is, "Behold, I make all things *Now*." All times, all seasons. All loves, all pain, all understandings. All work. All revelation. All humming of typewriters and snapping of briefcases and wielding of shovels and scalpels and opening and closing of books and washing of laundry and hugging of children and sorting of mail, and all assessment of life at mid-career, and all holding of a wet finger to the wind to see what is going on.

What *is* going on? Do we persist, thinking persons that we are, in trying to make sense out of life? It is pretty certain that by middle life we have seen enough of both chaos and order not to be simplistic about it, to know that whichever we choose, there is evidence to the contrary. Perhaps our choice, too, is a matter of our conditioning—if ours is a history of stability, good health, maybe we choose to believe that life wills us well—that, as someone has said, "the universe is friendly." If ours has been a history of difficult upheavals, perhaps we choose chaos. Either one can be a posture of faith, and whichever we have chosen there will be loose ends that do not fit. Maybe one of the gifts of middle life is to be able to "give over" that, to absolve ourselves of responsibility to make everything fit together. So, we may see life as chaos and the examples of order that come to us as happy coincidence, as atypical. Or we may persist in trying to find a redeeming pattern in life, abstracting out the good things and putting the terrors into another category—I can't understand it but it must have meaning, somehow. We may even acknowledge, begrudgingly, because we know our tragedies are real, not to be placated, that the worst things may have hidden within them something that may help us. I recall in Camus' novel, *The Plague*, that the townspeople knew the plague had ended *when the rats came back!* Good meanings in evil events. "Pain is the fire," someone has written, "that hollows out the cup that holds the rich wine of joy," and, almost against our will, we know that that, too, can sometimes be true.

We object to this somehow—it seems exploitative of tragedy, to "make something good" out of it, to cut off too soon our rage at the reality of evil. I recall being in a hospital room an evening after the birth of my second son when a woman was wheeled in to occupy the other bed. She had just delivered a child but the child was dead. The doctor was trying to tell her, in her drowsy state, that the child had died at birth and, in response, she said, in a sleepy, thick voice, "Well, the Lord giveth and the Lord taketh away—that's how it is," and the doctor, out of his powerlessness and anger, had said—to himself it seemed to me, as much as to her—"That's *not* how it is. Someday we'll know how to take care of these things, but we don't now." And I remember being torn between my feeling that if it was a comfort to her to think of her infant's death with this resignation maybe he should not jostle that for her, and on the other hand my gratitude to the doctor for being unwilling to gloss over this loss or to resign himself too easily to the unacceptable outrage of this infant's death.

We can, of course, nurse our grief, brood over it too long, until, years after the event, it still takes up all the landscape of our lives. "You could put the meaning of original sin this way," says Robert Capon. "Given a choice we would rather sulk than rejoin the party." Somewhere between these extremes we must find our place in relation to the tragedies that come to us.

Perhaps, depending on our nature and the circumstances of our lives, we can deal with joys and tragedies as they come and put aside conjectures about the ultimate meaning of life until either we have more evidence or, if death is the end, our questions die with us. Maybe it is a matter of no particular urgency to us—maybe we can wait. That was my position, too —I would trust life, trust God, enjoy what I had and leave the disclosures of overall meanings to the future. It is still, of course, all that we can do, if we need irrefutable evidence to show us where to stand.

Yet it will not do for me any more, that suspended judgment. Not since my daughter's death. Nor will it for many of us, facing the particular demands our lives take on at middle life. We need to weigh that evidence, make some kind of integrating conjecture about what it is our clues are pointing to. I see my daughter one day last spring, standing by the glass wall in the room where I write and saying to me, "I wouldn't mind dying young. It would be kind of keen, in fact." I remember the shock of it. "Mary!" I said. "Life is gorgeous. One world at a time." She demurred again, in a strange eagerness, I thought, to be on with it. Within a few months she had died and looking back at that time I ask myself, Did she know? Did she have some sense of it? And—the week before she died—I see her, looking down a table at me and smiling and saying, "I've had a full life already." Did she know? It has a terrible urgency for me now—the meaning of our experience—and I count over

113

my pieces of evidence like a miser hoarding her jewels. It is not a ho-hum question. Is there, in fact, something going on?

I have come to the technicolor section of my story—my own bits of evidence—halting, suspect, elusive—that at the heart of the universe there is Good News, that the Secret at the middle of life is a good secret. "We dance around in a ring and suppose," writes Robert Frost, "But the secret sits in the middle and knows." Of course we who are Christians have heard all our lives that the secret is a good one, and that the story of Jesus is the secret revealed. Yet we need to appropriate it for our own, to find our own small and terribly important evidence, in the evenings and the mornings of our lives. Faith and personal history. Our hunches come not from different events that, in our rational moods, we piece together into some kind of coherence. But perhaps they are the same cards, flipped over in the opposite direction, making bowls into faces, and tulips into shoes. Or maybe it is like the famous picture in which one sees an outlined vase and then sees that the sides of the vase are formed by the profiles of two persons, looking at each other. Our perceptions are shaken—the earth appears flat—but it is really round!

I have other pieces of evidence—many of them connected with my daughter's death, that something more than we had imagined is going on, not in some distant Order Room, but here, in the interplay of energy and event, in intuitions we have that go beyond what we can observe with our senses. I think of the lines of a song my daughter had copied on a slip of paper: "If I should leave you, try to remember the good times, warm days filled with sunshine and just a little bit of rain," or of the poem she had written on a scrap of paper that we found in her suitcase the day after she died ". . . You'll see what I mean When I shatter into thousands—You've never been so scared in all your life, And never so rewarded." That strange painting she worked on so intently just before the close of school—it did not come to me until weeks after her death from a head injury—It is a painting of a damaged head.

I read in a magazine article that appeared during the month that my daughter died, an excerpt from a book, *The Challenge of Chance*, by Arthur Koestler. The excerpt deals with various phenomena of extrasensory perception, a field in which I have long had an interest and some experiences to tell about, when people exchange such stories—eagerly, but shyly, because we do not want to be fools. I recall my daughter's psychic gifts—of how one evening she had been wishing for her friend to come but it was his study time and she did not think she should disturb him, so did not, but combed her hair and went downstairs anyway as though for a visit and of how in a few moments he showed up at the door and his first words to her were, "You called me, didn't you?" The thesis of Koestler's book has been described as being "Everything in the universe hangs together," and looking for some sense in all the meanings of our tragedy, I read of how it is believed there may be some kinds of anti-matter that travel faster than the speed of light and therefore, according to orthodox relativity theory, it may be possible for the knowledge of events to reach us before the events occur. Yes, I think, it could be, remembering her standing there saying, "It would be kind of keen, actually." Did she know? Did some unconscious knowledge surface from time to time—in her words to me, in her writing, in that painting? I know she was not afraid. I think she did not expect to die. I know she was happy on our vacation together—"I am having the time of my life," she wrote to a friend.

Something going on. Why did the beads I had associated with her since a happy weekend together last spring—why did they break in my hand the first time I put them around my neck after her death? Why did her brother's watch stop at the moment of her fall?

And what was it that came to me that August morning out there by the clothesline when the leaves on the bush in front of me shook for those moments in the still air and I was suddenly in some utterly new way lifted out of my grief and experienced a wholeness, a joy, a sense of being loved and known, that with all my experience of love and joy was new to me, a kind of undeflected ecstasy? So that when on several occasions I have read of persons who have been thought dead and then returned to life and they have tried to describe the feelings they had in that interim, I have read their words with recognition and thought, Yes, out there by the bush—that's how it was.

What is going on? Is there, at the heart of the universe, a

Love, a Design, so grand that we cannot even understand its terms, but of which we catch intimations, here, now, and promises of life to come? Elisabeth Kubler-Ross tells of her conviction after working with the dying that death is "the final stage of human growth." She tells of a woman, clinically dead, who, while experiencing a fantastic peace and wholeness, watched the frantic efforts of a resuscitating team to bring her back to life and who tried, according to her account, to tell them it was all right—to let go. The woman tells how she finally gave up trying to reassure them and then—these are her words —"I left consciousness." "Left consciousness"—to return to life? Can we conceive of it—we who are so aware of our own consciousness, our joy and our pain? Are we but numbed and blinded creatures compared to what we shall someday be? We who are Christians have heard this before, though even among Christians, certainly among liberal Christians, speculation about life after death has not been very popular of late years. "Live in the today," we tell each other. "There is work to be done. And love to be experienced. And there are daisies, and moonlight, and the taste of cold orange juice in the morning." And we are right. But then something terrible comes to us and we need more. There have been terrible things all along and in our lifetimes we have seen enough—the Holocaust, the burgeoning famine, the grinding down of poverty, the machinery of our nation running amok toward war and we seemingly powerless to control it. Have we not needed more then, too? Of course. But the death of my daughter is intimately mine. Our tragedies—and by middle life we all have them—wrench our agenda into urgent boldface type.

So we need more, and we remember the stories that may help us—Jesus, thought to be dead, his friends gathered round in their despair and suddenly—a sense of him, his presence, there he is! Something happened. Paul on the road to Damascus, struck down by—what? heatstroke? a vision? epilepsy? The poet, Theodore Roethke, writing how, at a low point in his career, he was visited by the poet, Yeats, long dead:

> . . . Suddenly, in the early evening, the poem, "The Dance" started, and finished itself in a very short time . . . I felt, I *knew*, I had hit it. I walked around, and I wept; and I knelt down—I always do after I've written what I know is a

good piece. But at the same time I had, as God is my witness, the actual sense of a Presence—as if Yeats himself were *in* that room. The experience was in a way terrifying, for it lasted at least half an hour. That house, I repeat, was charged with a psychic presence: the very walls seemed to shimmer. I wept for joy. At last I was somebody again. He—they—the poets dead—were with me.

Now I know, there are any number of cynical explanations for this phenomenon: auto-suggestion, the unconscious playing an elaborate trick, and so on, but I accept none of them. It was one of the most profound experiences of my life.[1]

Or my friend, writing from far away to tell me how, on a late spring day, visiting a remote New Hampshire farmhouse where they had spent time together, she had been overwhelmed by the return of grief over the death of her son many months before. Then she had experienced his presence again, some mysterious "joy of communion" in the song of a bird. "From that time on," she writes, "although there are moments of great loneliness and longing, I have been sustained by that experience and warmed by the knowledge that nothing can separate me from his love."

I add my own stories. Our friend who on hearing of our daughter's death called us long distance in great distress, and then called again late at night, and then the next night he called again—he could not rest, it was too much for him. "I don't understand it," he said. "I haven't even known her that well lately. We hadn't seen each other for years." On the next day he called again. "I canceled my classes this morning," he said (he is a college teacher). "I have never done that before. But," he went on, "Mary is with me."

"Tell me about it," I said, hungry, wanting to believe it.

"She came suddenly," he said. "She has been with me. She knew I needed her. It is very warm, like a blanket. Something is going to be heard."

What is it I find in his words—a willing suspension of dis-

---

[1] Ralph J. Mills, Jr., ed., *On the Poet and His Craft: Selected Prose of Theodore Roethke* (Seattle: University of Washington Press, 1965), p. 24.

belief? Yes. How like her, I thought. She was fond of him. And she loved to go to people who needed her. "I believe you," I said. "It could be so."

I think of my birds. "Feed the birds . . . feed the birds. . . ." The song goes through my head until, half in impatience to get past it, I put out the seed, scattering it on the snow-covered patio. And then, hours later, in a wave of desolation, turning from my desk to look out the window, I see there, hopping about, pecking at the seed, my red cardinal and his mate, and suddenly my heart is light. He stayed with me for a very long time—hopping to a low branch and dropping down again, so close to my window. They have come at other times, appearing through a low windowpane, or in a high tree, when I have needed them.

Does it seem far-fetched to believe in the revelation of love because a bird comes to my window or because, in my back-yard, I am transported, through the trembling of a bush? "Unless all existence is a medium of revelation," writes Archbishop Temple, "no particular revelation is possible." I wonder what tiny exploding personal event in his life he was trying to legitimize as revelation when he wrote those words. The ultraviolet light cast on the stone. The stone itself, broken open to reveal the interior crystals of a geode, never before this moment, this moment of our cracking of its skin, seen. The bread broken open . . . "And their hearts leapt within them." Something going on.

Faith and personal history. Faith and middle life. What have we to tell, to bear witness to the light? Or to the darkness, for that matter, and, God knows, we have seen that, too? Only our own stories. We do well to be cautious, about laying our stories on other people who were not there. What on earth will they think?

Yet we need to tell them, too. Paul, writing to the church at Corinth, says, "I must boast; there is nothing to be gained by it, but I will now talk about visions and revelations given me by the Lord." Then he goes on to tell about being snatched to the highest heaven, about visions, about not knowing whether it happened outwardly or was just in his head but it doesn't matter—in either case God did it—"this man was snatched to Paradise."

Coming across these words, sitting in a seminar where we have been discussing Paul's life and work, I am struck almost physically with a sense of recognition. I have not been that fond of Paul, finding him a turgid and dogmatic man, and an anti-feminist, too. But as I read the words, the centuries and cultures between us collapse into a single frame, and I see him, trying to throttle down his excitement so his audience will not think he has gone crazy. (One can see his hearers wince a bit, avert their eyes—Now really, Paul—"visions"? "snatched to Paradise"?) So, all right, he says, and goes on to talk about what his friends can observe to be so, about his thorn in the flesh and about Titus coming to see them. But I know that what keeps him going in the night, and through rejection and pain and prison, what sets his heart to dancing, is his story—that once, fourteen years ago, he was "snatched to the highest heaven" and "there he heard things which cannot be put into words." It is his story, outlandish as it may be, that moves his life.

It is our stories, too, our histories, that move our life beliefs off some page so they enter into the daily ebb and flow of our life. It is out of our history that the love of God comes to us, in response to whatever needs our lives lay upon us, in response to getting up, going to bed, to death and to joy, to news pictures in the paper and calls on the telephone and all the many terrors and marvels of our lives.

"The love of God"—Are you crazy? I can hear someone say, and I have said it to myself times enough, wondering how I can accumulate so avidly my pieces of evidence that something good is going on when, on the other side of the balance scale, sits a weight heavier than almost anything I can imagine. And I can only say, my shoulders heavy with the weight of it, I do not know. Maybe some day I will understand it all—though even that seems facile to me now. A friend writes to me, about our belief that "God is love." "I trust God only because I have no other choice . . . and I have to be freed over and over to believe that God is love. We have grown up with that expression and forget how much evidence there is against it. In facing Mary's death you have no doubt had to face the question, Is God love? I don't know, but like Pascal I have to bet on that because there's no other hope."

What frees us, to believe that God is love? Only what works for us. Daniel Berrigan writes about his experience with prayer in prison: "I have discovered two things about prayer since entering prison: first, that when I pray humbly and honestly I can hack this life even at its bitterest. When I don't pray, I cannot.

"When I don't pray I begin to apply to life the only power I really know—violence. Inch by inch I begin to disintegrate, and so do my relationships with others. I begin to brood over the injustice of this experience, and the dark side of my soul assumes control. But when I pray, I accept my dependency on God and on my friends. And a love not my own is lent me. And I can continue."

Does it mean, this sense of being visited by a love not our own, that we shall be free of loneliness and grief? No. I see, after a long absence and then only for a few hours, a friend with whom I share a common grief. We have talked and now it is time for me to go and she, her grief being older than mine, and wanting to help me with what is ahead, says to me, "It doesn't get any better. But—" she hesitates. I frame the sentence for her—"There is great richness in it?" She nods, "Yes, there is."

Out of our experience, out of what brings us healing and light our faith comes to us.

So, I believe in the incarnation, in the presence of God in our common life, because in the flesh, and voice, and vibration, and aura of people I love, I find love, and healing and great joy. I believe in the fellowship of the Holy Spirit, the kingdom of God, because when I have been despairing, people in my religious community have put their arms around me and held me close. And when I have been joyful, they have done the same. And because I have been in gathered rooms where a mystery has been present and its nature has been Yes. Humming with Yes. Bursting with Yes.

I believe in Jesus because I need a form into which to put all the best hunches we have about what people can be to one another, and because I need a person to voice the message to me: a story of risk that paid off, though not right away, not in the way anyone expected; a message of a love that will never draw the line and say, You have pushed me far enough

—that's all I can take, but of a love that says, instead, Whatever you are, that's what I love, and if you let me love you I will make you whole. And if you won't, I will love you anyway—it is the one thing you cannot have from me—any hope that I will not love you. And I believe in Jesus because once as a child, lying awake full of anxiety and distress I heard inside my head the words, "Let me have it," and my image of who that was who offered to take it was Jesus, and I gave over my care and went to sleep. And because a few times in my life I have been moved to an act of will to relinquish and the image of Jesus has been a good receiver. In a sermon, I hear a minister say, "No one who touches the hem of his garment is unaffected." And I remember walking down a city street with my daughter when she was small and for some reason was going through a stage of being afraid of clouds and wind and how on this day the sky darkened and the wind blew and I wrapped the front of my wide blue coat around her and she held to the side of my skirt and was not frightened any more and we walked down the sidewalk together, a four-legged creature under a strangely billowed coat. The hem of my garment. The hem of his garment.

And because when I hear the words of a song, "Oh, when dark-ness comes . . . and pain is all around, Like a bridge over troubled water I will lay me down," I think, Yes, the incarnation of Jesus—and what we, you and I, are to each other.

We are Christ to each other. So I further believe in Jesus because once, in a foreign country, as I stood in the lobby of an auditorium milling with thousands of people, and feeling stricken and alone in my personal tragedy, a man I knew but not well came up and put his arm around my shoulder and said to me, "Someone loves you. God loves you. And Dorothy and I love you," and then he went on to say how, working in the office with my husband and knowing of our need he had tried to stay close, without being intrusive, and now he wanted to tell me, too, of his love for us.

And I believe in prayer because something has upheld us through the long winter and when a friend who has cared for my mother writes to me and says, "Whenever I say the Rosary, I say extra prayers for you," it comes to me—Maybe that is why. Maybe the hundreds of people who have said to us, "We are praying for you," are not only giving us the affirming love of that moment and the memory of it, but something in the energy they release as they fulfill their promise—"We will pray for you"—reaches to us to surround us with help.

And I believe in eternal life because I need to, and because my mother tells me how her mother on her deathbed greeted her loved ones who had gone on before and because I read of the latest work of Elisabeth Kubler-Ross, and because a friend tells me how, sitting alone in a church, playing at the organ, he was visited, several months after her death, by the presence of a young woman, a presence so strong that after awhile he stopped playing and said, "All right, Mary Beth." And then, he tells me, "I *felt* her smile." And because, standing by my father's bedside as he lay dying I had for an instant a sense of adventure and gladness that startled me, as though he was about to set forth and the news of that voyage was good news. And because something happened to the disciples after Jesus' death, and because my daughter, with all her psychic gifts, believed in a life beyond this, and because something came to me in the backyard of my house on an August noonday.

And I believe that everything in the universe hangs together because on a road in the high mountains of Colorado as our sons and we were out driving in a dull automaton way a few days after our daughter's death, a car pulled in front of us and the son who was driving said, "Do you see the bumper sticker on that car?" On the car was a sign none of us had ever seen before nor have we since, and the words of the bumper sticker read, "Mary Is Our Hope"—a sign put out by a Roman Catholic church nearby. But why then? why there? And because my birds came.

And I believe in Powers, God the Power, God the Lover, moving among us because one night in desolation, feeling my daughter's loss as though it were all fresh, I heard the phone ring and a young woman who is like a daughter to me said, "This is Catherine. How are you?" and I said, "Why did you call?" and she said, "I was sitting here, and I just thought of you," and perceiving my distress, she said, "Are you alone?" and I said, "Yes," and she said, "I'll be over in a few minutes," and she came.

"Unless all existence is a medium of revelation . . ." writes

William Temple. What was it he was talking about? Had a bird come to him, or a bush trembled? Had a friend called? Did he, in some gathered group, experience, as a surprise, the holy community? Had he happened to read something that jumped from a page—or a car—and called his name? Had he seen a signal mirror—flash, flash—come to him from the top of Estes Mountain? Did he feel, suddenly and at last, at home with himself? Had his work fallen into place—his life, after long struggle, assumed the pattern of Now, of this holy moment, whenever it is, wherever you are, whatever your hand and heart and mind find to do?

Theology begins with a cry, or a lump in the throat, or some gladness we do not know what to do with, or with some intimation of meaning we do not fully understand. And it continues in the morning and the evening of each day's life, in shadow and sunlight, and in the high noon of each one of us.

Epilogue

It is now almost six years since my daughter's death. It is five years since this book was finished and began its journey as my proxy into the larger world.

Were I writing the book today, it would surely be different, though its perceptions and its hopes still seem authentic. I would stand by them all. I am grateful for that—that I did not, in the desperation of my need, believe then what I can no longer believe now.

I am still "middle-aged." Five years doesn't change that. I have recently given up the part-time job that helped me through these years—giving me a daily community, a different place to be, different things to think about than those inner realms in which a writer wanders. I work at home now, can write for long hours and relish the freedom of unstructured days rather than viewing them with panic. I have written other books and, I hope, shall do more. I still swim at the neighborhood YMCA and have met in its chlorinous waters people who have read my book and, knowing where I live, have speculated they might find me there among their swimming companions.

My husband and I continue to work with our grief, to miss our daughter, from time to time to weep for our loss. But the balance of that has shifted, though it did not happen right away. At first a kind of pervasive sadness was the "norm" of our lives, and the good times, the joyful times, were the exception. Now it is the other way around. I am grateful for that.

I am grateful for this book. It has made me many friends among those who have seen in my journeys some echoes and reflections of their own lives. Even as I have been helped by the journeys of others I am glad to pass the story of my own along. The writing of the book certainly helped me work my way through dark times, brought me great joy in the discoveries it helped me make, as well as in those moments of a writer's elusive but exhilarating triumph: that sense of absolute congruence between what is felt and what is written. I am glad to have the book as a record of who I was then, and of the people I loved.

The change of title, to *The Growing Season,* was my idea. It is probably more fitting now than when the book was first published. It would have been suitable for the middle life aspect back then, but for the grief aspect, perhaps not. It might have implied too soon the presence of a silver lining, as one resents a well-meaning outsider saying in the aftermath of tragedy, "You'll be stronger because of this." *Don't tell me that,* the heart cries out, *I want none of it.* To say this is somehow to sanction the loss, to leave it and the one who is lost behind.

I have not left my daughter behind. Wherever else she is, she is surely not back there. Someone has said that a child who has died is with us always, as a living child can never be. In some ways I have found this true, though to say it glibly or as any kind of acceptable substitute is to deny the reality of loss. I am not recompensed, but that is not the point. What is added, what is gained, is in a way on a different sheet from what is lost. So I have learned to be grateful for the enrichment and confidence and faith my loss has brought, while accepting also, as an element of life, the sadness that is a given with me as much as the earth, the air, my sense of humor, my confidence that I am loved.

We are all, the people in this book, proceeding with our lives. My husband and I, jolted, for a time all but shattered, by this event, have grown closer. I am grateful for that; it might have been otherwise. As middle age demands new attention be paid to leftover, unresolved issues as well as to its own agenda, so does the death of a child, and all of this may be too much for a marriage to bear. Marriages get worse or they get better; they do not stay the same.

The three sons revealed on these pages have moved further into lives and relationships of their own. We rejoice in their independence and their closeness. The image of Estes Cone—of the adventurous young people flashing their signals from the mountaintop and then coming back to tell us how it was—has been borne out, with the pleasant variation that the parents, too, have had their adventures and come back to tell their stories.

We are all more aware of the suffering of others, more able to help. We gravitate toward those who have suffered a similar loss as toward members of a family. In grief there are many who are alone, but there are no strangers. So our lives are enriched and strengthened by that bond of knowing and being known.[1]

My daughter's death is no longer the chief agenda of my life, as for a while, it surely was. A bereaved father, writing in *The Christian Century,* says of his child's death, "It is a vacuum that sucks all meaning into itself."[2] In time, the energy poured into grief moderates, distributes itself over the rest of life, too— sometimes, it seems, almost against our will. To begin to forget is to be startled with fresh pain at each remembering. But there is something else. In the burning intensity of early grief, symbols are everywhere—one's sense of God never farther than a breath or a page away. We see, as William Blake said, "a world in a grain of sand . . . And eternity in an hour." As the sharpness of grief fades, so may the daily symbols of transcendence. My birds—my cardinals—still come, but our meetings are more casual now. Do I miss that—reading the meaning of the universe in such personal terms? Sometimes. But it's all right with me, this steadier, underlying faith, still in the ready, I hope, for revelation, though the wind needs to blow a little stronger now—as a burn that has begun to heal no longer feels every slight shift of air that passes over it.

So, I have invested myself in life again. It is a reciprocal thing, for life has also drawn me to itself—in the trust and love of family and friends, in work in which I can lose and find myself, in the community of faith which proclaims and acts out its story, telling me again and again who I am and who I have chosen to be, and in the mysteries of all faith and all knowledge, which seem endless, and sometimes call my name. My daughter, too, calls me into life, as I have felt her blessing and encouragement in some of the ventures of these past years, as I feel her with me now, and as I move toward her through the rest of my life, confident that we shall be together again.

But I move through life differently, with a fuller awareness that, certainly by middle age, to fully commit one's self to life one must, in some kind of life-permeating fashion, have come to terms with death. Not that we will be free of anxiety and pain,

---

1. An organization of bereaved parents was begun in England and now has chapters in many cities in the United States. For information, write: Compassionate Friends, 800 Enterprise Drive, Oak Brook, IL 60521.

2. George C. Spratt, "Waiting for the Light," *The Christian Century,* May 21, 1980, p. 567.

but that beneath all of that will be some sense of confidence, of unshakable strength. To the extent that I feel that in myself, I am grateful.

My mind returns to a scene on the day after our daughter's death. A loved friend had come to be with us. She walked into the room where we were and came and put her arms around my neck and said, "Everything's going to be all right."

For her to say that to me then seemed the most incredibly rash statement I had ever heard. And, for a moment at least, I believed her.

Six years have passed and I am far, in geography and mood, from that anguished room. It is still a rash promise. Yet, in greater tranquillity now, and aware of the ambiguities and mysteries in which we live, I venture to say it myself, in the words of the fourteenth-century Christian mystic Juliana of Norwich: "All shall be well, and all shall be well, and all manner of thing shall be well." Or, in a more tentative mood, to quote the words of a more recent sister writer, Emily Dickinson:

> Hope is the thing with feathers
> That perches in the soul
> And sings the tune without the words
> And never stops at all.